AF539096

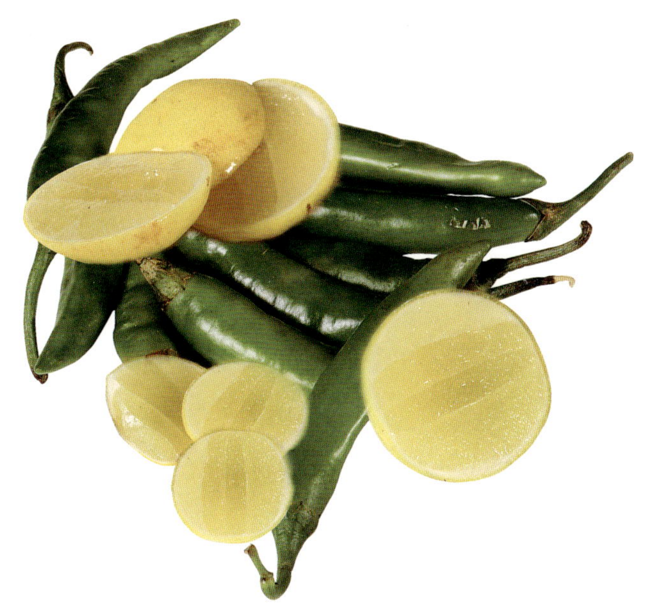

CUISINES

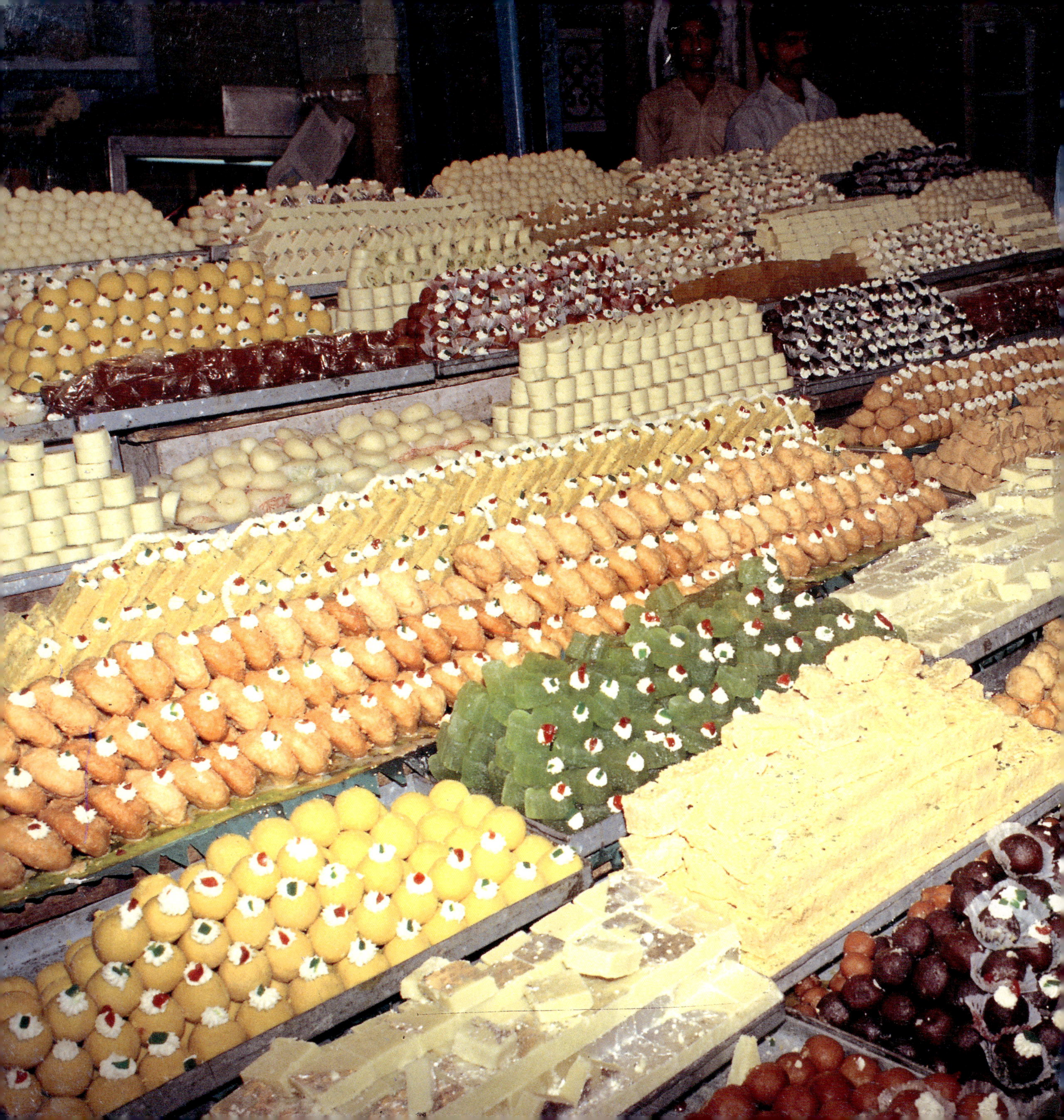

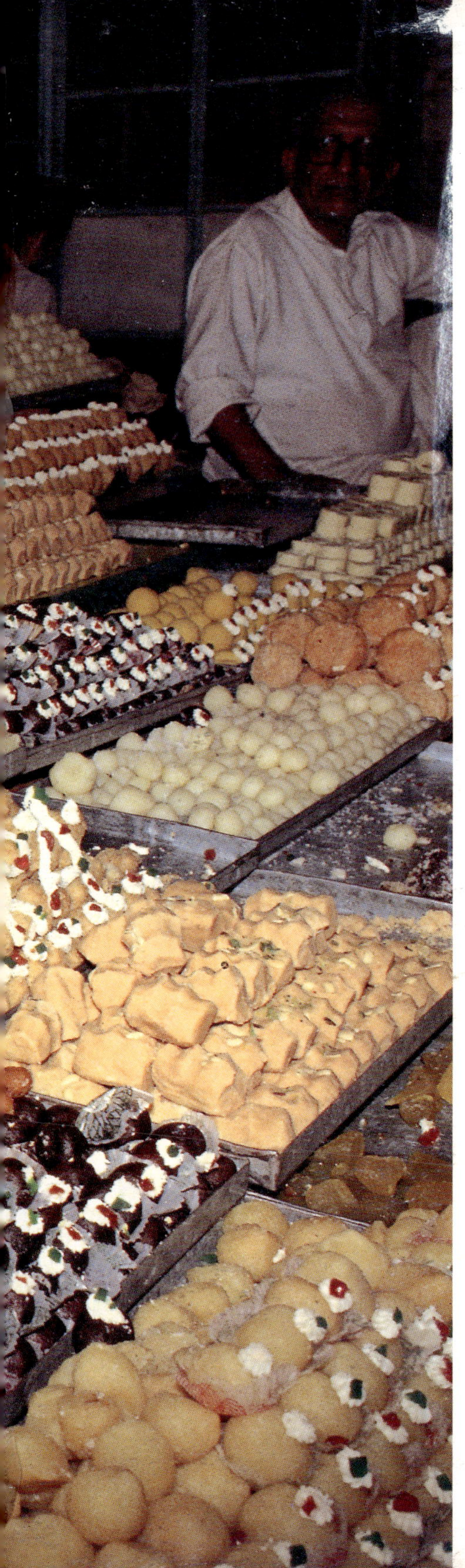

Incredible !ndia

CUISINES

Text Pushpesh Pant
Photographs Anuj Parti

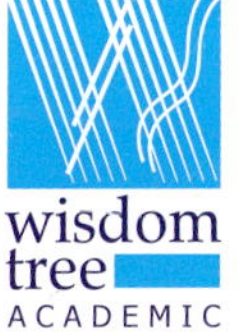

By arrangement with
Department of Tourism, Ministry of Culture, Government of India

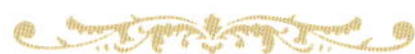

To the fond memory of my mother
Jayanti Pant nee Pande,
brilliant teacher and fabulous cook
who showed me the way,
then left me free to explore on my own
rivers with their waters tranquil or turbulent

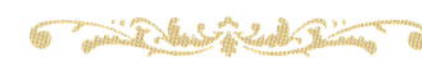

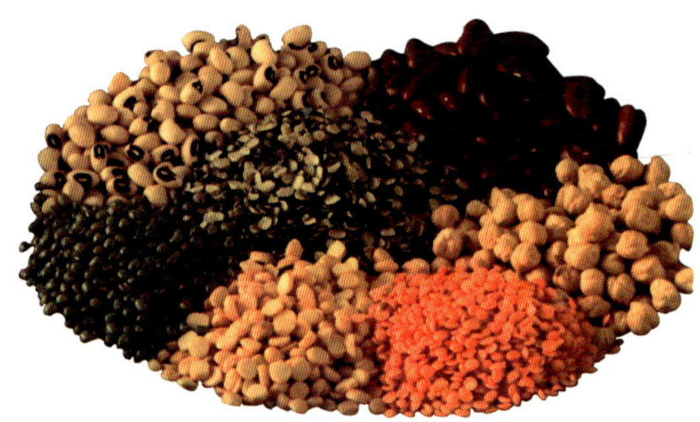

Published in 2007 by

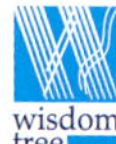

Wisdom Tree
4779/23 Ansari Road, Darya Ganj, New Delhi-110002
Ph: 23247966/67/68

Photo credits: Anuj Parti, Amit Pasricha-page 39; Ashok Dilwali-19,33; Phal Girota-29; Incredible India-6,9,13,14,49; National Museum-10

Recipe photographs courtesy:

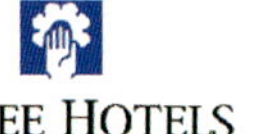

JAYPEE HOTELS
You're among friends...

ISBN 81-8328-072-2

Conceptualised and published by Shobit Arya for Wisdom Tree; *edited by* Manju Gupta; *designed at* SN Graphix and *printed at* Print Perfect, New Delhi - 110064

Preface

The cuisines of India are best visualised as a magnificent river system crisscrossing across the sub-continent, uniting different regions — food zones — with indissoluble links. One must resist the temptation to identify the mainstream or get carried away pleasantly by the powerful flow of mighty rivers. Be it Mughaliya-Punjabi-Awadhi-Hyderabadi, Bengali, Chettinad-Tamil Brahmin, Malayali-Malabari, Goan-Mangalorean-coastal, Kashmiri or Rajasthani-Gujarati vegetarian, the evolution of different regional and ethnic styles and gastronomic traditions immediately recall the metaphor of the journey of a river from its source to the sea.

What lends a unique enchantment to the 'whole' is the fascinating interplay of tributaries and distributaries. The confluences dramatically highlight the ongoing process of synthesis that is so characteristic of Indian civilisation; no less significant is the contribution of a culinary waterway shifting its course. Sudden influx of effluent — an exotic produce, a new crop or a cooking technique introduced by an itinerant trader-merchant, scholar-pilgrim, or soldier-adventurer — has often triggered or helped this process. What starts as a small pristine trickle from the glacial melt in the snow-capped Himalaya becomes a swollen torrent, with much alien stuff in its bosom, as it tumbles along its way, meandering whimsically, standing still (dammed) at times, always sustaining life, spreading joy and occasionally springing some surprises before it merges with the ocean.

Those who dwell along the banks of these rivers naturally enjoy an intimate personal bond with the waterway they consider their own. It gets entwined with the sorrows and joys of everyday life, local fairs and festivals, an integral part of their identity. So is it with cuisines. This, however, does not mean that the river belongs to any individual or a parochial group. All great rivers, as well as small streams hidden in unexplored wilderness admit affectionately into their family and fold all those who fall in love with them.

Cuisines of India should be approached in the same eclectic spirit. There is nothing mysterious or terrifyingly exotic to deter the uninitiated. Foods and flavours of India are accessible to anyone interested and can be enjoyed by everyone like its music, dance, literature and majestic monuments.

The book *Cuisines* showcases in an incredibly delicious manner the synthesising genius of the people on this sub-continent — the capacity to balance the native with the foreign, classic with the folk, gross with the subtle and ephemeral with the eternal.

Pushpesh Pant

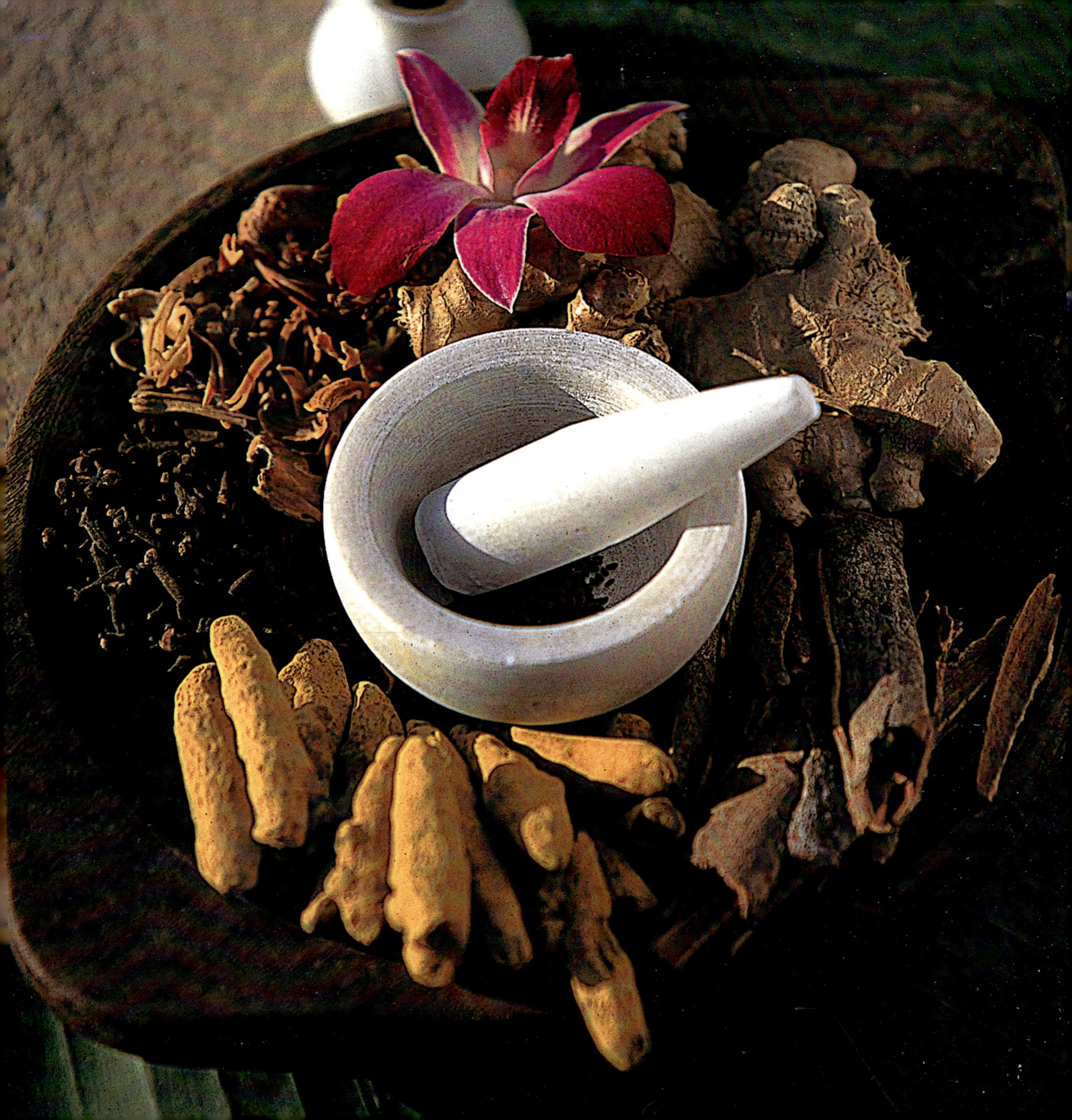

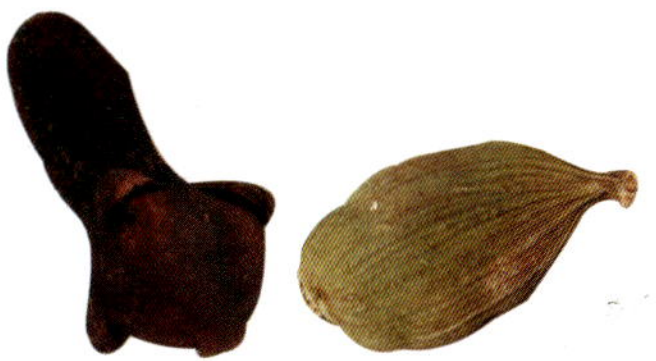

Contents

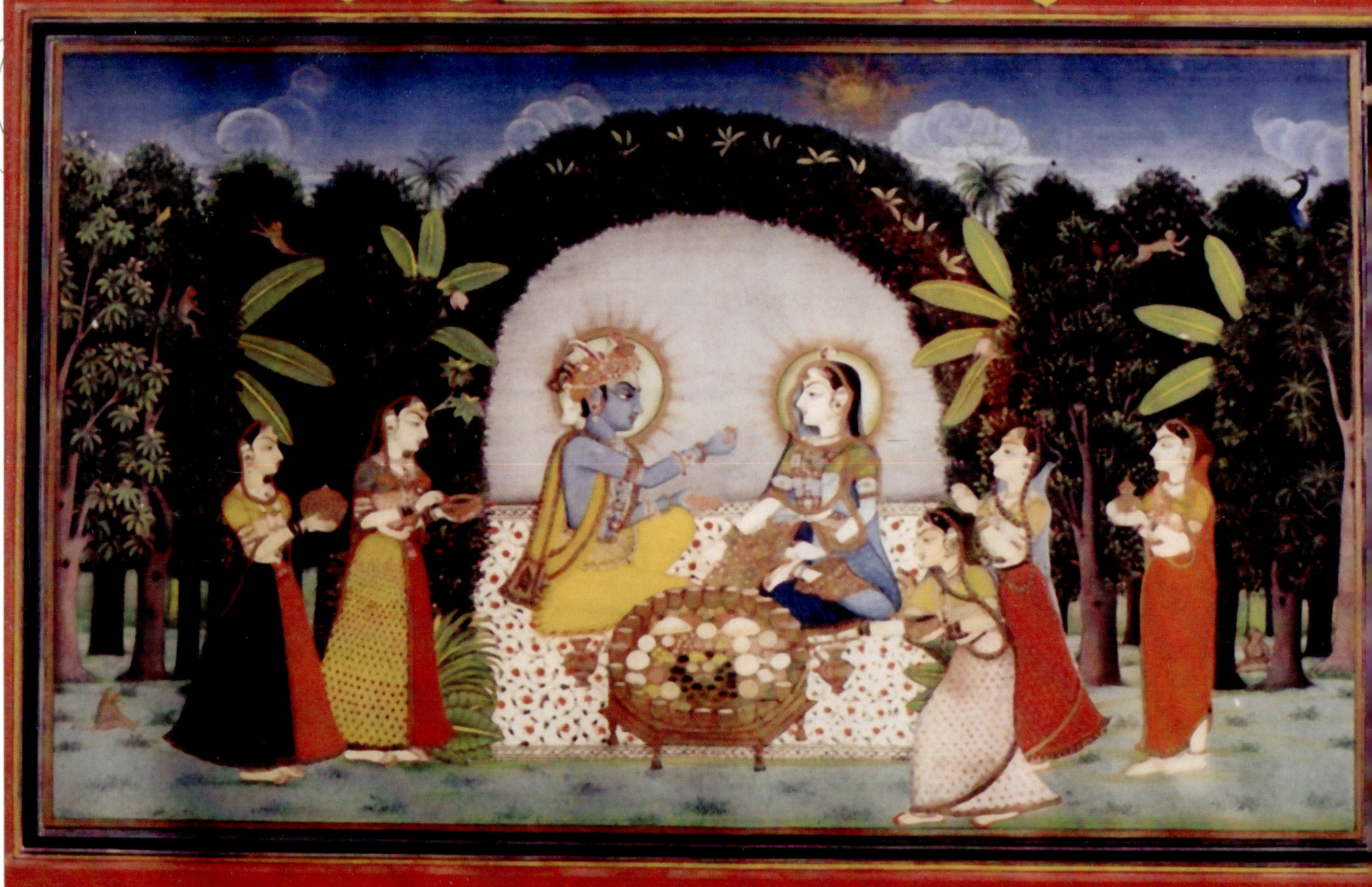

The national identity of people is defined as much by their cuisine (and costume) as by the language and literature, arts and artefacts. Both cuisine and costume are governed by taste. Taste, in turn, reflects the intrinsic temperament and acquired preferences. Both are inextricably intertwined with the personality of an individual and the community. Food and dress are intimately related with prescriptions and prohibitions, acceptable or unacceptable, and their study allows us to learn of the unique genius of a civilisation more effectively. It goes without saying that both these topics are interrelated and their interaction with technology and trade has often changed the course of history. The cuisines of India hold a bright mirror that reflects the attainments of the Indian civilisation in a refreshingly different manner.

The culinary and cultural heritage of India illustrates the harmonious blending of diverse influences over the centuries. Nothing displays the synthesising genius of our land better than the evolution of Indian cuisine. Not only have the different regions of the sub-continent interacted with one another through the ages and influenced each other's foods, flavours and fashions, but also kept their doors open to external ideas and welcomed novel cooking techniques and exotic ingredients brought by the outsiders.

The basic tenets of Indian thought are reflected in India's culinary philosophy — the concept of *satvik, rajasik* and *tamasik* foods which is matched with three different personality types in the famous spiritual text, *Shrimad Bhagwat Gita*. These three terms roughly correspond to spiritual, active and inert materials respectively.

Later Ayurvedic texts compiled in the first millennium after the birth of Christ introduced and refined the concepts of *guna* and *dosha*, which are intrinsic properties of ingredients used in food and the basic humours in the body. The three *doshas* — *kapha, pitta* and *vata* were in turn related to the natural elements like space, earth, water, fire and air.

Equally important in this context is the concept of *shadras* — the six

LEFT
This miniature painting depicts Krishna offering a delicacy to Radha from the chhappan bhog *(56 dishes) laid out by the maids*

basic tastes, namely *madhur* (sweet), *lavana* (salty), *amla* (sour), *katu* (bitter), *tikta* (pungent) and *kashaya* (astringent). It is amazing how perceptively the six basic tastes were related to the six seasons. The great poet Kalidasa has painted moving word-pictures of the cycle of seasons in his lyrical work, *Ritusamhara,* wherein he often refers to 'the golden grain ripening in the fields' or some 'luscious fruit stoking the fire of love'. To date we crave for seasonal delicacies, like savouries in the monsoon and sweets during winters. Come summer and the scorching sun sends us scurrying for thirst retardants and coolants. It is interesting to note that Ayurveda refers to many of the 'summer' spices as *trishna nigrah,* the thirst retardants. Ingredients prescribed for the winter months are *balavardhak* (tonics). Many Mughal miniature paintings depict seasonally appropriate food with the characters portrayed while eating and musicologists have always laid great emphasis on the right *raga* (melodic form) matching the season and the time of the day. All that Ayurveda advises you to do is to pay similar attention to your food. Swing with the season and match your mood.

By the beginning of the last millennium these ideas filtered down to the grassroots and were deeply embedded in popular consciousness. Individual temperaments and inclination were balanced with the surroundings of the natural environment. Indian cuisine in different regions of the sub-continent has evolved through centuries guided by this holistic philosophy that laid great emphasis on living in harmony with Nature.

It may be said with conviction that Indian food is the key to understand the lifestyle of Indian civilisation. Indian foodlore enriched with Ayurvedic concepts is inseparable from the fairs and festivals held to celebrate the seasons. Recapitulation of the story of the evolution of Indian cuisine allows us to appreciate the aesthetic and scientific accomplishments of the Indians for the past thousand years and more.

RIGHT
A young girl majestically ensconced on a pile of corncobs

Commenting on Indian cuisine, the late litterateur-cum-gourmet extraordinaire, Dr Rahi Masoom Raza once observed that "a dining table is

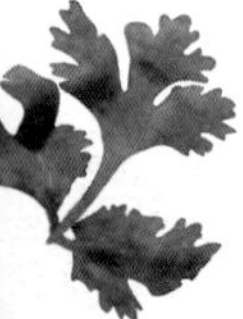

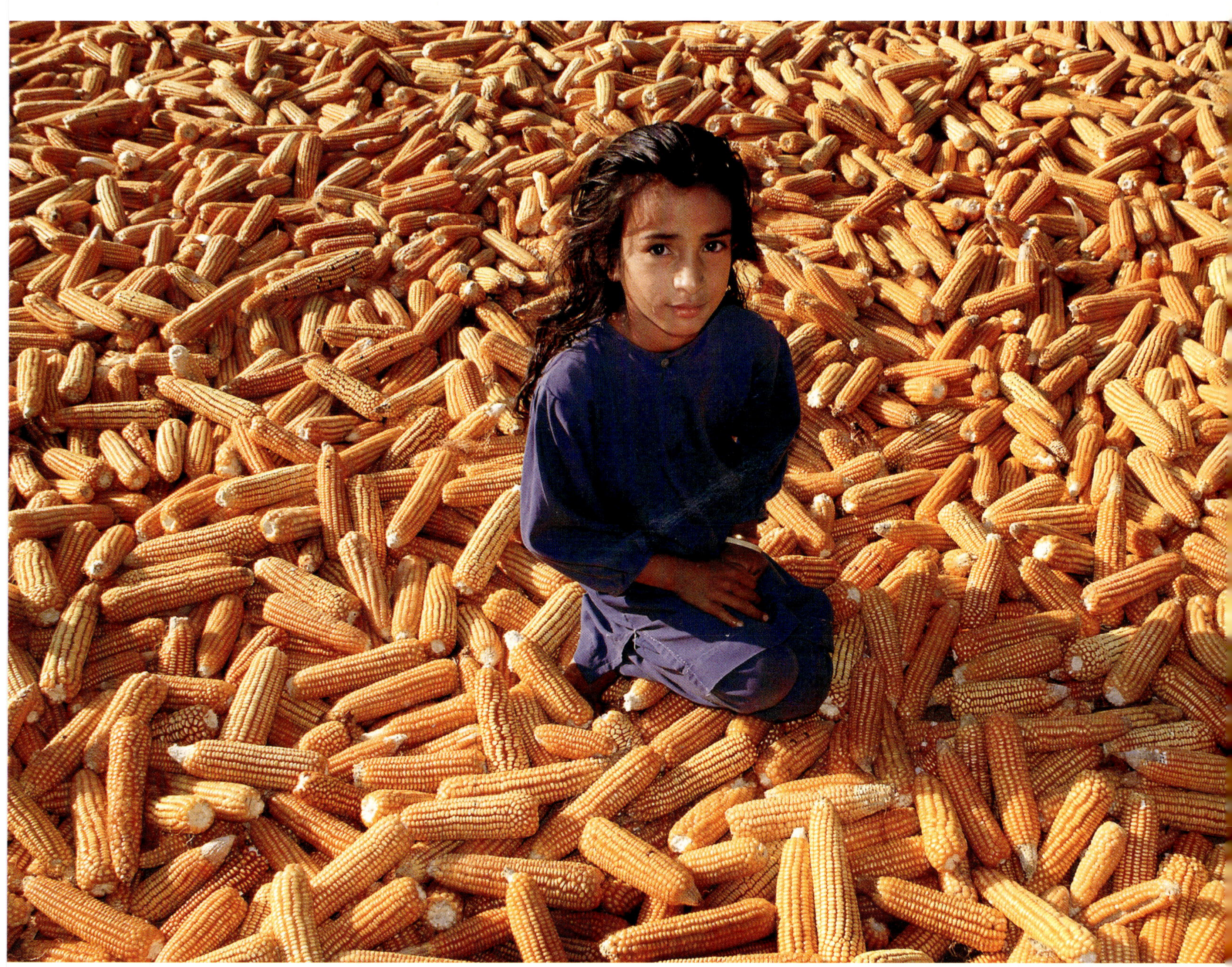

lured a particularly villainous demon. When he began to torment the villagers, they implored Sage Kashyap, the ascetic who was in meditation on its banks, to save them from his wrath. An equally disturbed Kashyap cast a spell to vanquish the intruder. He drained the lake's waters by creating a depression on its western side and the valley thus born was christened *Kashyap-mar*. It was, eventually, distorted to *Kashmir* or *Cashmere*.

Situated at the crossroads of Asia and touching the historic Silk Route, Kashmir has imbibed a diversity of cultural influences emanating from Central Asia, Persia, Tibet and the sub-continental mainland. Kashmir, which came under the sphere of Mughal influence, experienced a renaissance. Emperor Jehangir (17th century) loved Kashmir and retired to the Vale for his summer sojourns. The gourmet that Jehangir was, prompted him to describe Kashmir as a 'paradise on earth'. He introduced saffron to the Mughal *dastarkhwaan*.

When the Mughal power declined, and the Afghans gained ascendancy, they brought with them their culinary preferences. Many of them took root to give birth to the Kashmiri penchant for *dumba* (ram) and *kabargah* (deep-fried spare ribs). As a reaction to Afghan misrule, the Kashmiri populace welcomed the Sikh intervention. Maharaja Ranjit Singh appointed his favourite military commander, Gulab Singh, as the Viceroy. Not surprisingly, the Punjabis, too, influenced Kashmiri cuisine. The Kashmiri *waazwaan* today reflects a blend of Persian, Central Asian, Afghan and the Punjabi streams.

It has been said that Kashmir is one-third water, one-third mountains, one-third land. The beauty of the land is breathtaking. Water bodies not only provide fish, but are also their most prized 'farmlands'. Here they harvest *nadr* (lotus stems) and *haaq* (a variety of spinach) which are the mainstays of Kashmiri vegetarian food.

RIGHT
Branches of an apple tree weighed down by luscious apples

On the upper reaches are the *marg* or flowery meadows: Gulmarg, Sonemarg and Khilanmarg. Just below the meadows are the orchards

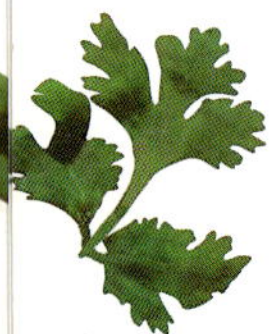

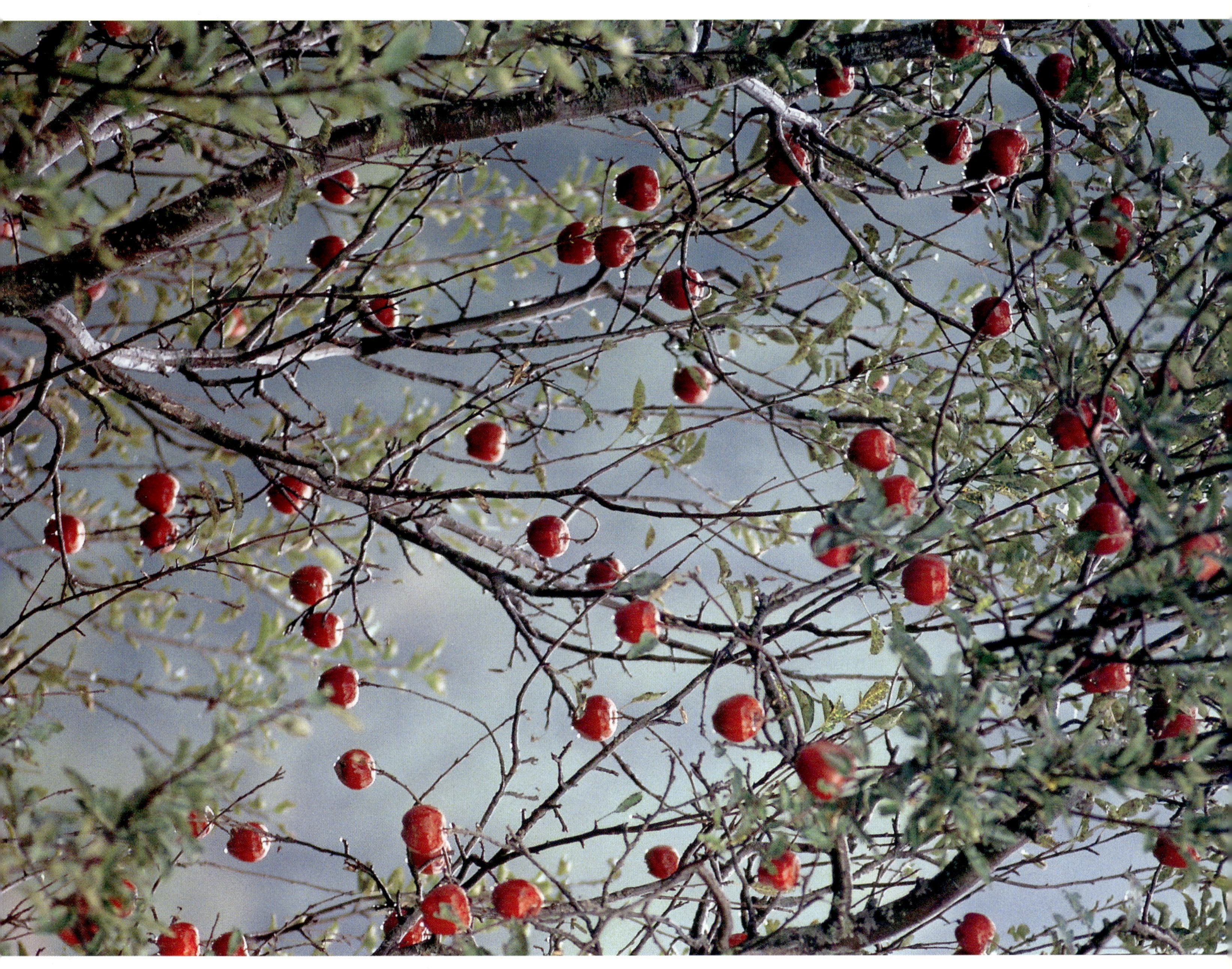

fringed by forests of silver oak and birch. Apple, cherry, peach, pear, plum, *loquat*, almond, walnut and pine nut abound and enrich the table of the rest of the nation.

The Valley itself is resplendent with carpets of saffron. In Pampore, near Anantnag, the fields of this burnished gold extend as far as the eye can see. The name 'Pampore' is derived from *Padmapur*, the Lotus City. The lotus, in this case, refers to the sublime saffron flower. Saffron or *kesar* is also referred to as *kumkum* in Sanskrit and was traditionally applied as an auspicious mark on the forehead.

The saffron from Kashmir enriches delicacies like *kesariya* in the southern states of the Union and is generously used in the sublime *biryani* and desserts of Awadhi and Hyderabadi cuisine. The Kashmiris in turn cannot do without the clove, cinnamon and the cardamom grown in the southernmost tip of our land (in Kerala) to add flavour and fragrance to their *waazwaan*.

The concept of *waazwaan* is unique. The term *waaza* means 'cook', and *waan* means 'shop'. The traditional *waazwaan* consists of 36 courses, though eating a 20-course meal is more the norm. It is said that the host must lay out all the food available in the kitchen before the guest, and the guest, on his part, must reciprocate the gesture by doing full justice to the meal.

People sit in fours, as it is considered auspicious to share a *tarami*, the Kashmiri version of the *thali*, which allows one to sample the best of the *waaza*. The *tarami* is a large, ornate plate that comes covered with a filigreed copper dome to keep the food warm. It arrives heaped with rice and the first few courses. Each successive course follows separately to allow the enjoyment of a distinct flavour. The crowning glory, *ghushtaba*, constitutes the last course.

Kahwa is served last from the *samovar* and it leaves behind lingering memories of the *waazwaan*.

Ghushtaba

INGREDIENTS

500 gms fatty meat
5 cups/1 litre hung curd
½ cup/100 ml *ghee*
4 cup/ 800 ml stock
8 green cardamoms
6 black cardamoms
6 cloves
3 tsp fennel powder
3 tsp dry ginger powder (*sonth*)
3 tbsp/45 ml garlic water
1 tbsp onion paste (fried)
½ tsp dry mint leaves
Salt to taste

METHOD

- Pound the pieces of mutton with a wooden mallet, adding small amounts of fat, a pinch of *sonth*, salt, and black cardamom till the meat is crushed to a silken texture.
- Shape the minced meat into balls of about one-and-a-half inch diameter. Boil water in a thick-bottomed pan and place these *ghushtaba* pieces in the pan.
- Add the *ghushtaba,* cooked curd, *ghee*, and stock and heat to bring to a rapid boil. Add the green and black cardamoms, cloves, fennel and dry ginger powder. Cover the pan and continue to boil for 10-12 minutes.
- Now add the garlic water with salt and boil for another 10 minutes. Add more hot water, if required, to maintain a soup-like consistency.
- Add the onion paste and salt. Cook until the *ghushtaba* is tender (spongy) to touch and the gravy has thickened. Sprinkle the dry mint leaves over it before serving.

Nadr Yakkhni

INGREDIENTS

1 kg lotus stems (cut diagonally into 1½ inch pieces)
1.5 litre water
4 black cardamoms

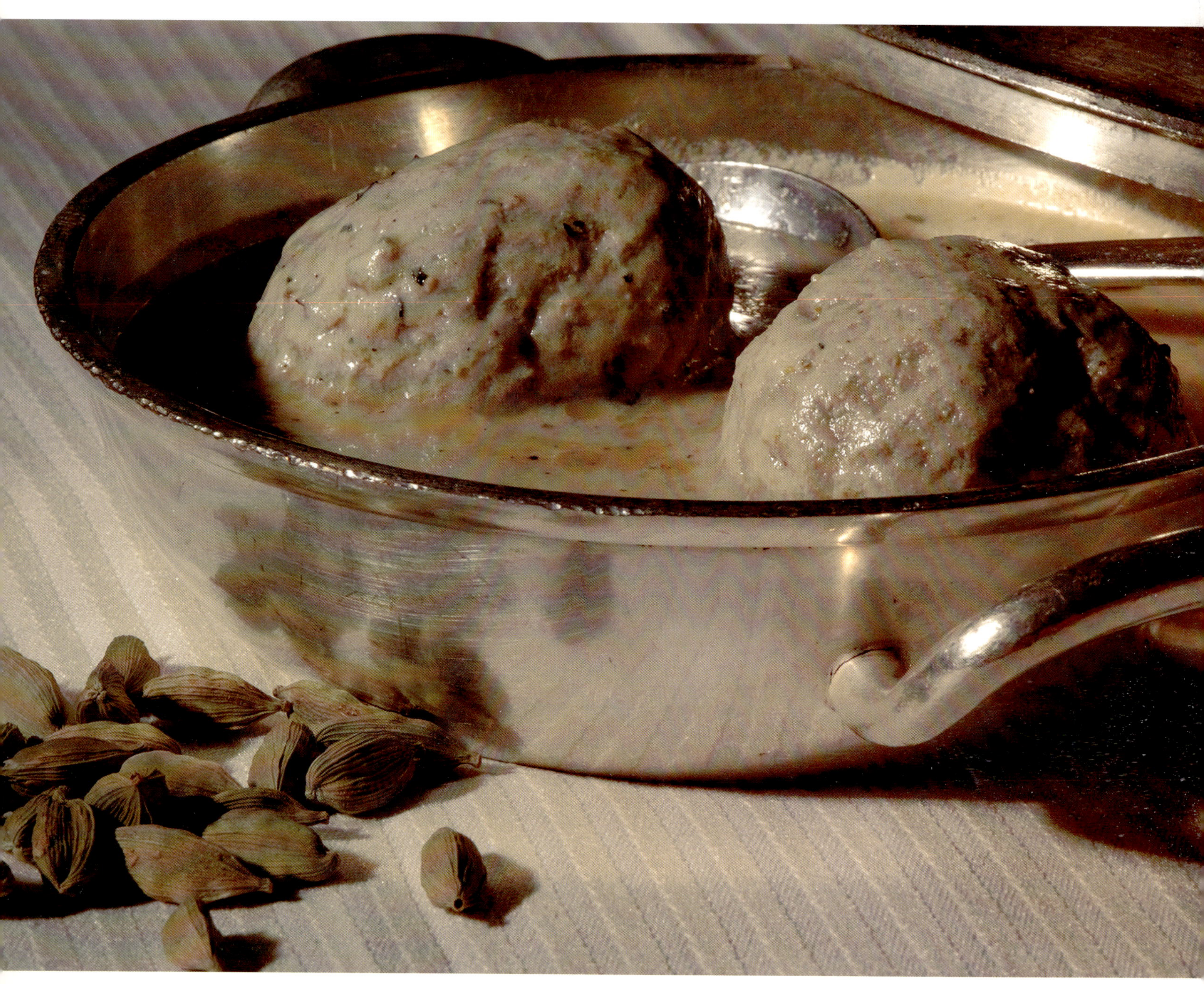

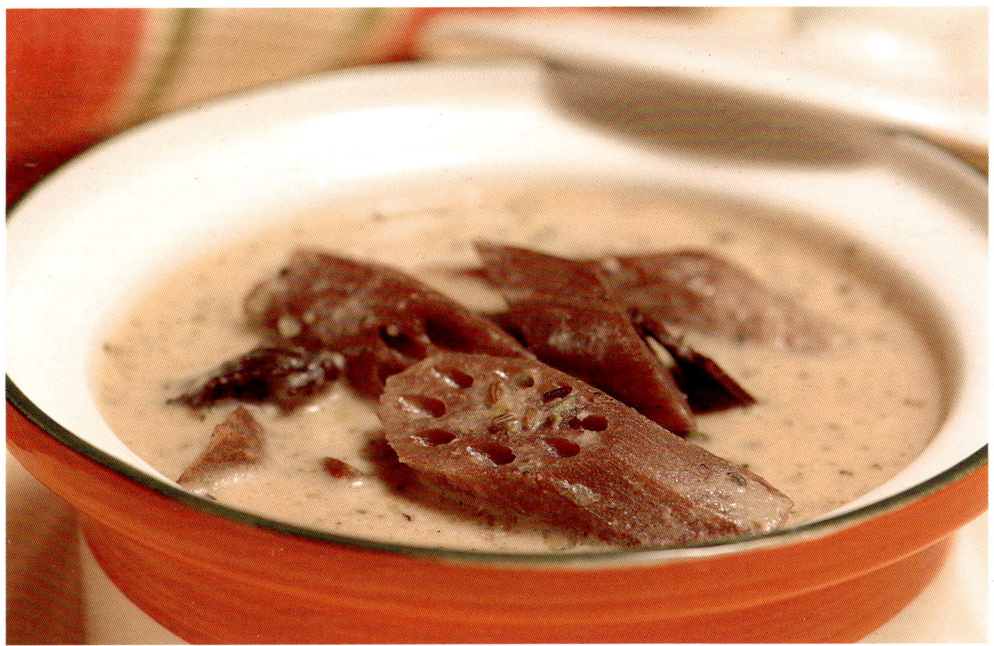

8 green cardamoms	2 tsp dry ginger powder
8 cloves	2 cups cooked curd
4 cinnamon sticks, 1 inch long	½ tsp dry mint leaves
⅓ cup *ghee*	½ tsp black cumin seeds
2 tsp aniseed powder	Salt to taste

Method

- Boil the water, add the lotus stems, and cook them until half done.
- In another pan, add the black and green cardamoms, cloves, cinnamon sticks, *ghee*, aniseed powder, dry ginger powder, cooked curd and salt. Stir well and cook for about 10 minutes.
- Add the half-cooked lotus stems; reduce the heat and simmer till tender.
- Add the dry mint leaves and black cumin seeds. Mix well.

LEFT
Ghushtaba *balls floating in the appetising gravy*

ABOVE
Nadr yakkhni *constitutes part of the 20-course meal of a Kashmiri*

PUNJAB

Punjab, the 'land of five rivers', with fertile fields and rich dairy products has been the envy of rest of the sub-continent. Punjab, situated at the crossroads of the Silk Route, imbibed diverse culinary influences. Its proximity to Persia, Afghanistan and Central Asia gave it a taste for fresh and dried fruits and exotic nuts. Amritsar, famous for its Golden Temple, is equally renowned as a commercial centre. It was a cultural melting pot for caravans from Bukhara, Kabul and Kashmir as these landed here and provided an important outlet to Peshawar and beyond. The wonderful diversity of the frontier foods and the rich streams of Hindu, Sikh, Pathan and Kashmiri migrants have enriched the Punjabi cuisine. The people of this province have lovingly cherished and preserved their cosmopolitan taste and eclectic tradition.

Punjab has traditionally laid emphasis on robust food, prepared with the simplest of ingredients and the easiest of basic techniques. *Chanak* (*chana dal*) is very popular in the region and is stated to have reached India with Alexander the Great's troops, who came to India via Afghanistan.

The cuisine of Punjab was never monolithic. Once the largest state in the land, Punjab was subdivided into separate culinary regions, each with a distinct taste. There is the food of the Pothohar plateau (Rawalpindi and its environs), Peshawar (influenced by Afghanistan and Uzbekistan), Sargodha (famed for its sweets), Lahore and Amritsar (the traditional melting pots).

The Partition brought an unprecedented influx of Punjabi refugees who introduced the rest of the nation to a rich diversity of Punjabi food. A string of *dhaba* sprang up all over the cities and then proliferated along every single highway. They introduced to the nation the joys of *tandoori* cuisine and pleasures of eating out. The modern Punjabi is an intrepid traveller and an adventurous entrepreneur. In the course of his globetrotting, he has acquired the taste for the exotic. The contemporary Punjabi repast aspires to be subtle and sophisticated.

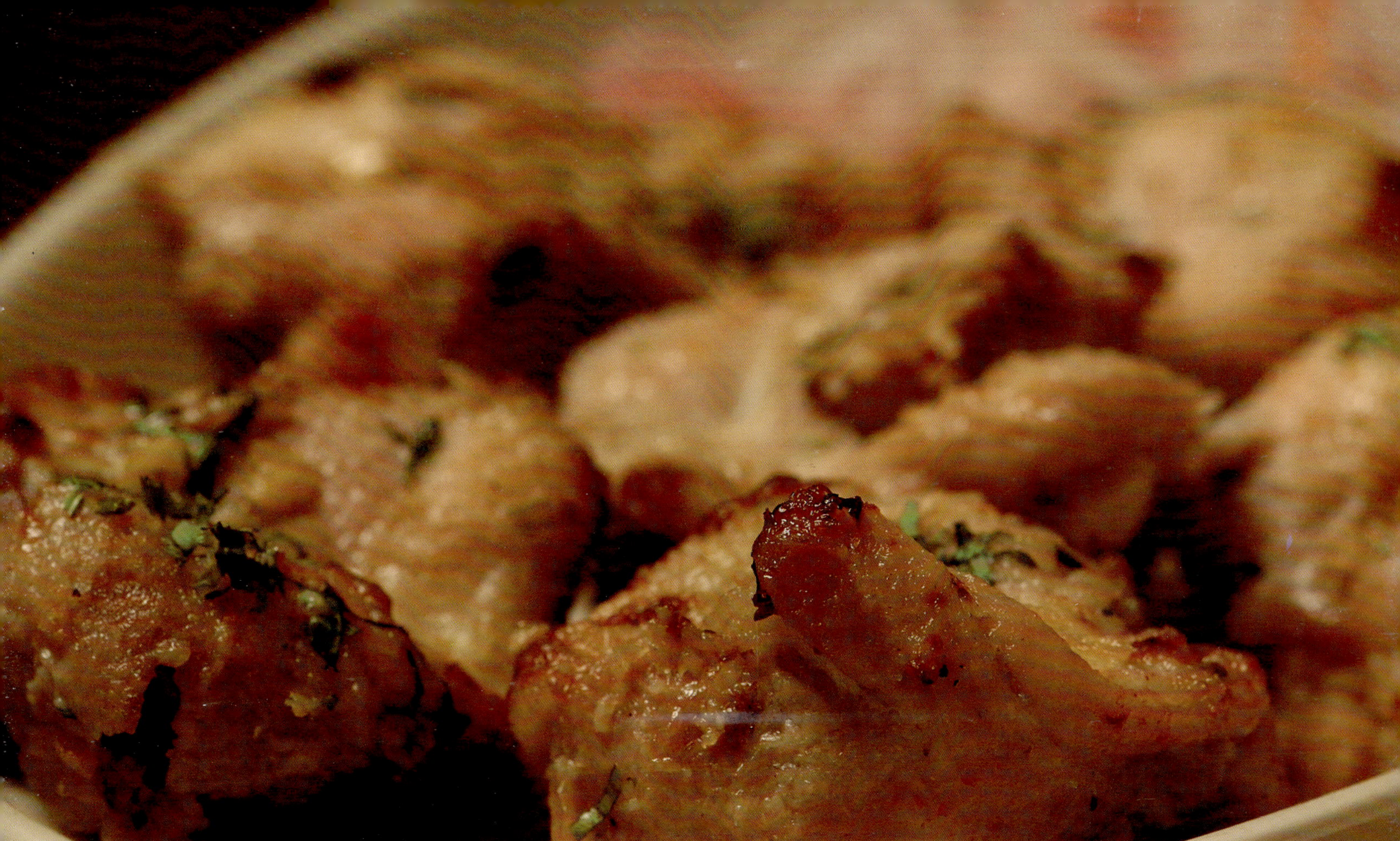

Murg Malaai Kebab

INGREDIENTS

12 supremes of chicken

FIRST MARINADE

2 tbs ginger paste (strain)
4 tsp garlic paste (strain)
¼ cup malt vinegar

SECOND MARINADE

1 cup hung curd
3 gm white pepper powder
½ tsp fennel powder
⅛ tsp cinnamon powder
1 tbsp coriander
½ cup cream
Salt to taste

ABOVE
A non-vegetarian Punjabi meal is incomplete without murg malaai kebab

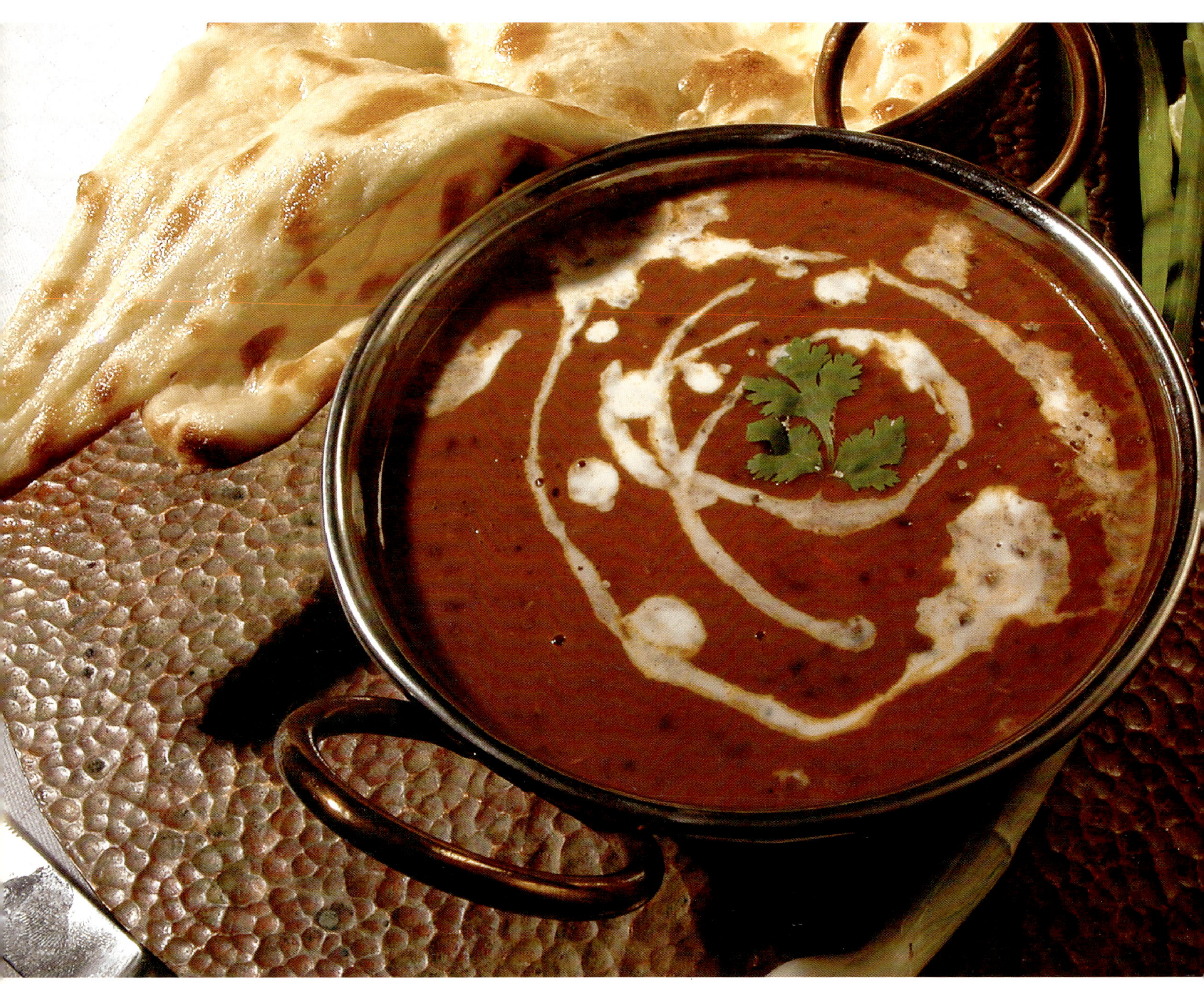

METHOD

- Clean the chicken from its bones and cut each breast into three equal-sized *tikka*. Wash and pat dry. Mix all the ingredients of the first marinade and rub the chicken pieces with it.
- Whisk curd cheese in a bowl. Clean, wash and finely chop the coriander. Mix coriander and remaining ingredients with the curd cheese, whisk and stir in the remaining cream. Rub the chicken pieces with the marinade and keep in the refrigerator for an hour.
- If cooking in the oven, thread three *tikka*s on wooden skewers and keep aside. If cooking in the *tandoor* or on a charcoal grill, skewer the *tikkas* and keep a tray underneath to collect the dripping.
- Pre-heat the oven to 350°F.
- Roast in a moderately hot *tandoor* for approximately four or five minutes or on a charcoal grill for about the same time. If using a pre-heated oven, baste with butter at regular intervals for six to eight minutes.

Dal Makhani

INGREDIENTS

1 cup *urad dal* (whole)
2 tbsp cooking oil
5 tsp garlic paste
3 tsp ginger paste
1 tbsp red chilli powder
400 gms tomato puree
200 gms butter (unsalted)
½ cup cream
Salt to taste

METHOD

- Wash and soak *urad dal* overnight and drain. Alternatively, boil the *dal* for a couple of minutes and reserve it in the same water for an hour and drain.
- Put the *dal* in a pan, add 3 litres of water and oil, bring to a boil and reduce to very low heat. Cover and simmer until cooked (for about four hours). Then add garlic paste, ginger paste, red chillies and salt, and continuously mash the lentils against the sides with a wooden spoon (for an hour).

LEFT
Dal makhani *forms part and parcel of every meal served on a joyous occasion in Punjab and Delhi*

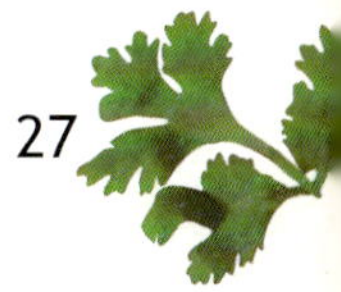

- Now add tomato puree and 150 gms of butter, and continue mashing the *dal* (for an hour).
- Stir in cream, and remove and adjust the seasoning. Garnish with the remaining butter.

DELHI

Delhi, the imperial capital for many dynasties, has drawn men of talent in diverse fields to seek their fortune here. This resulted in the city becoming a unique cultural crucible. Its cuisine incorporated the best of Hindu-Rajput, Bania and Kayastha communities as well as imbibed the Turko-Afghan and Persian-Mughal influences.

The Mughals dominated the political life of the country for more than two centuries and India enjoyed a long spell of peace and prosperity. Imperial patronage allowed various art forms to flourish. Great strides were made in the realm of gastronomy. The extension and consolidation of the empire led to evolution of a cosmopolitan culture and taste, and the administrative infrastructure made it possible for trade in different commodities to flourish. Such was the impact of Mughal interest in cuisine that till date the word 'Mughal' remains synonymous with Indian cuisine. It would be no exaggeration to say that an unprecedented and most exciting fusion of flavours was ushered in by this dynasty.

Mughal cuisine has a rich repertoire of *qorma*-braised meats served with a thick sauce-like curd-based gravy, *kaliya*, viands with thinner water or milk-based gravy and a multitude of *kebab* shallow fried on a griddle, like the *shami* or the *seekh* (skewered chunks of chicken or lamb) grilled on an open fire.

Delhi has a vibrant tradition of snacks and street foods, most of them vegetarian. *Chaat* is literally a moveable feast of tangy savouries 'prepared before your eyes' and dished out by the vendor from a portable kiosk, *khumcha*. *Berhvin poori,* stuffed and deep-fried puffed bread, served with *methi*

RIGHT
A chef displaying his skill in preparing the rumali roti

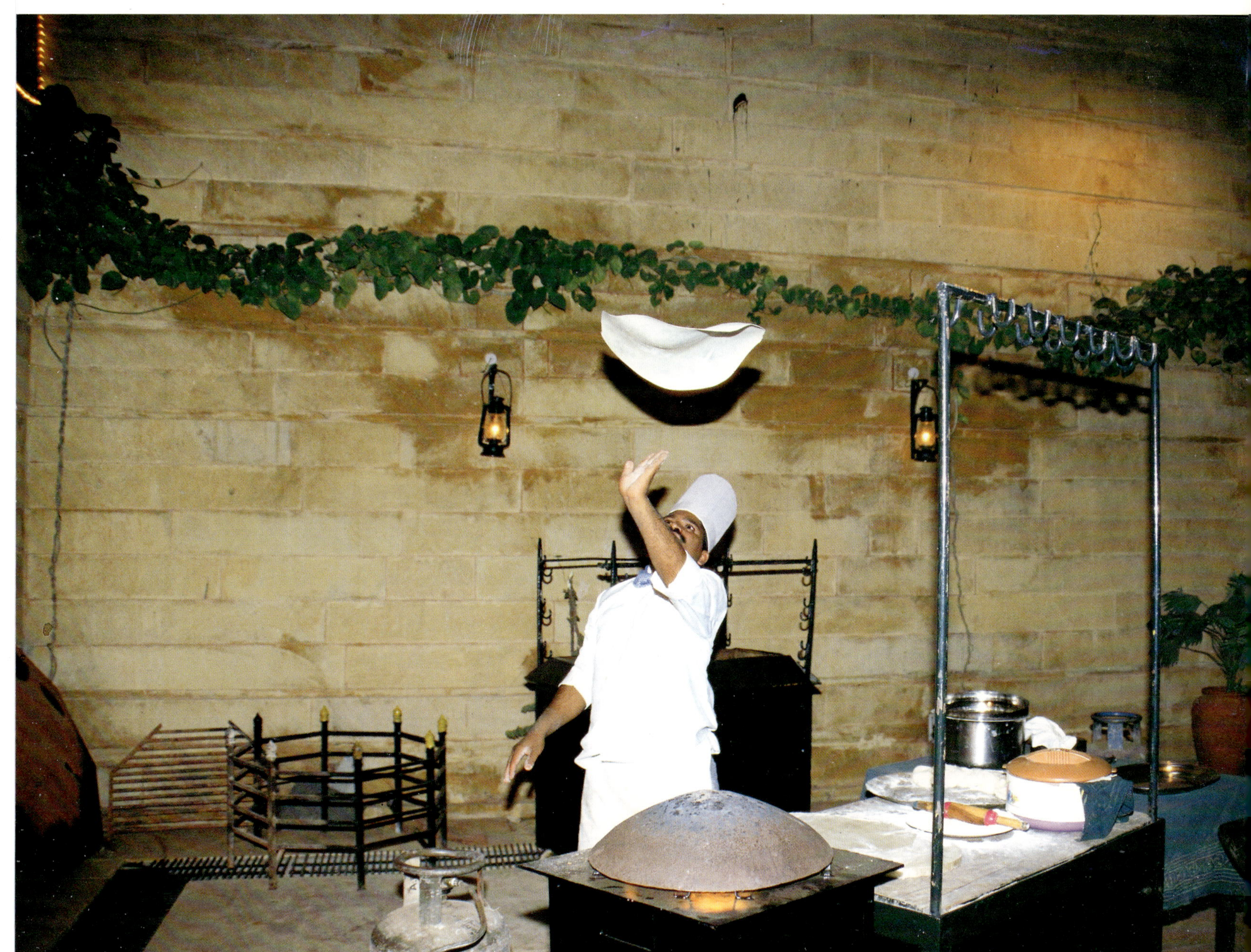

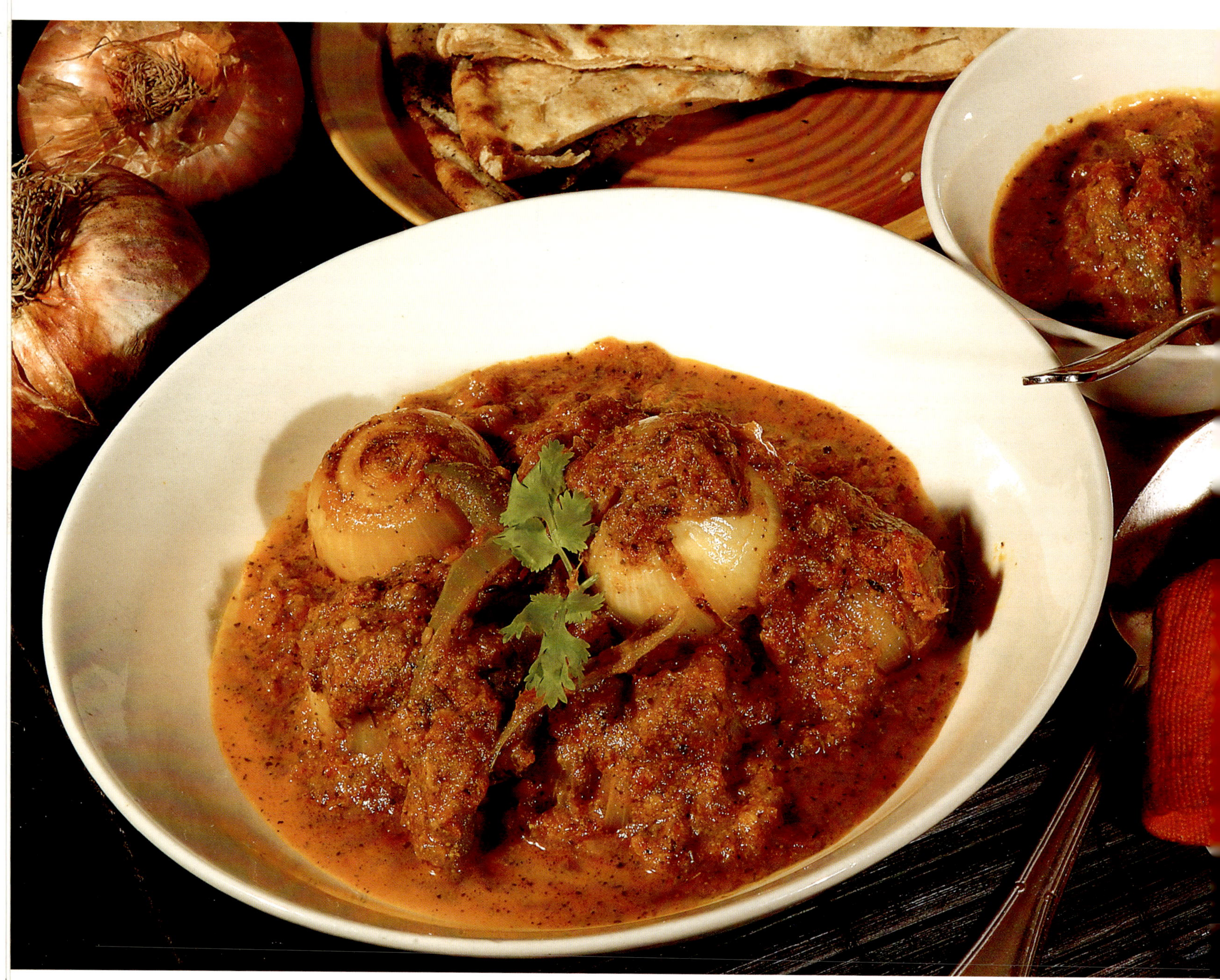

Kandey ki Sabzi

Ingredients

½ kg onions (medium/large sized)
1 tbsp coriander powder
3 tbsp oil/*ghee*
1 tsp turmeric powder
1 tsp cumin seeds
1 tsp red chilli powder
5 tsp garlic paste
250 gm tomatoes
1 tsp ginger paste
A pinch of *kasoori methi* (dried fenugreek leaves crushed between the palms)
2 green chillies

The Filling

1 tsp *amchoor* (dried raw mango powder)
½ tsp turmeric powder
1 tsp coriander powder
1 tsp cumin powder
½ tsp red chilli powder
Salt to taste
A pinch of black rock salt

Method

- Peel, wash and make criss-cross incisions on the onions for filling.
- Prepare the filling by mixing all the ingredients listed under this head.
- Pack equal quantities of the filling between the incisions in the onions and reserve for about 30 minutes.
- Heat oil in a pan, add cumin, and stir over medium heat until it begins to splutter. Add the garlic and ginger pastes.
- Stir and fry until the moisture evaporates.
- Add green chillies and stir-fry for a minute. Then add coriander, red chillies and turmeric (all dissolved in 3 tbsp of water).
- Stir for a minute, add tomatoes and stir while frying until the tomatoes are completely mashed.
- Now add the onions and salt. Stir, reduce to low heat, cover and cook, stirring occasionally until the onions are cooked, but are not squishy or soft.
- Sprinkle *kasoori methi*, stir and remove before attending to seasoning of the dish.

LEFT
Kandey ki sabzi *is specially relished in the desert region of Rajasthan*

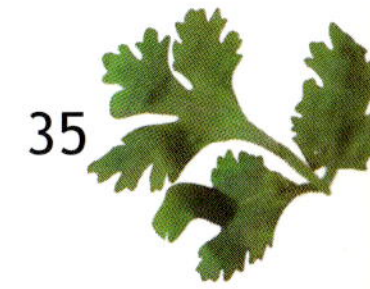

Bharwaan Gatte

Ingredients

Gatte

250 gm gram flour
3 tsp ginger (finely chopped)
1tsp baking soda
1 tbsp coriander (finely chopped)
60 gm curd (whisked)
4 tbsp *ghee*/clarified butter
Salt to taste

Filling

125 gm cottage cheese (grated)
2 green chillies (deseeded and finely chopped)
60 gm *khoya* (grated and cooked milk reduced to a pulpy form)
24 roasted pistachios
Salt to taste
10 gm ginger (chopped)
Ghee/clarified butter to deep fry

Gravy

100 gm *ghee* (clarified butter)
2 tsp green cardamom powder
1 tsp cumin seeds
1 tsp fenugreek seeds
¼ tsp cinnamon powder
1 tsp turmeric powder
2 cups curd (whisked)
5 tsp coriander powder
¼ tsp mace powder
2 tsp red chilli powder
A pinch of asafoetida
A pinch of fenugreek leaf powder
1 tbsp coriander (chopped)
Salt to taste

Method

- Sift gram flour, baking soda and salt in a tray. Add the remaining ingredients and 90 ml of water, kneading it to make a hard but pliable dough. Divide the dough into 24 equal portions.
- Mix all the ingredients and divide into 24 equal portions. Flatten the gram-flour balls, place a portion of the filling in the middle, make balls again and then shape them into croquette-shaped *gatta.*
- Heat *ghee* in a deep pan, add croquettes and deep fry over medium heat until light golden. Remove on absorbent paper to drain excess fat.
- Keep curd in a bowl, add coriander powder, red chillies and salt and

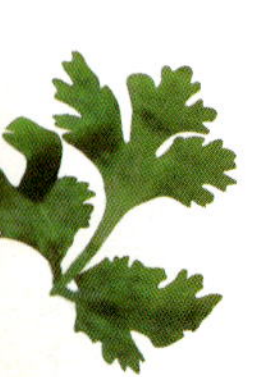

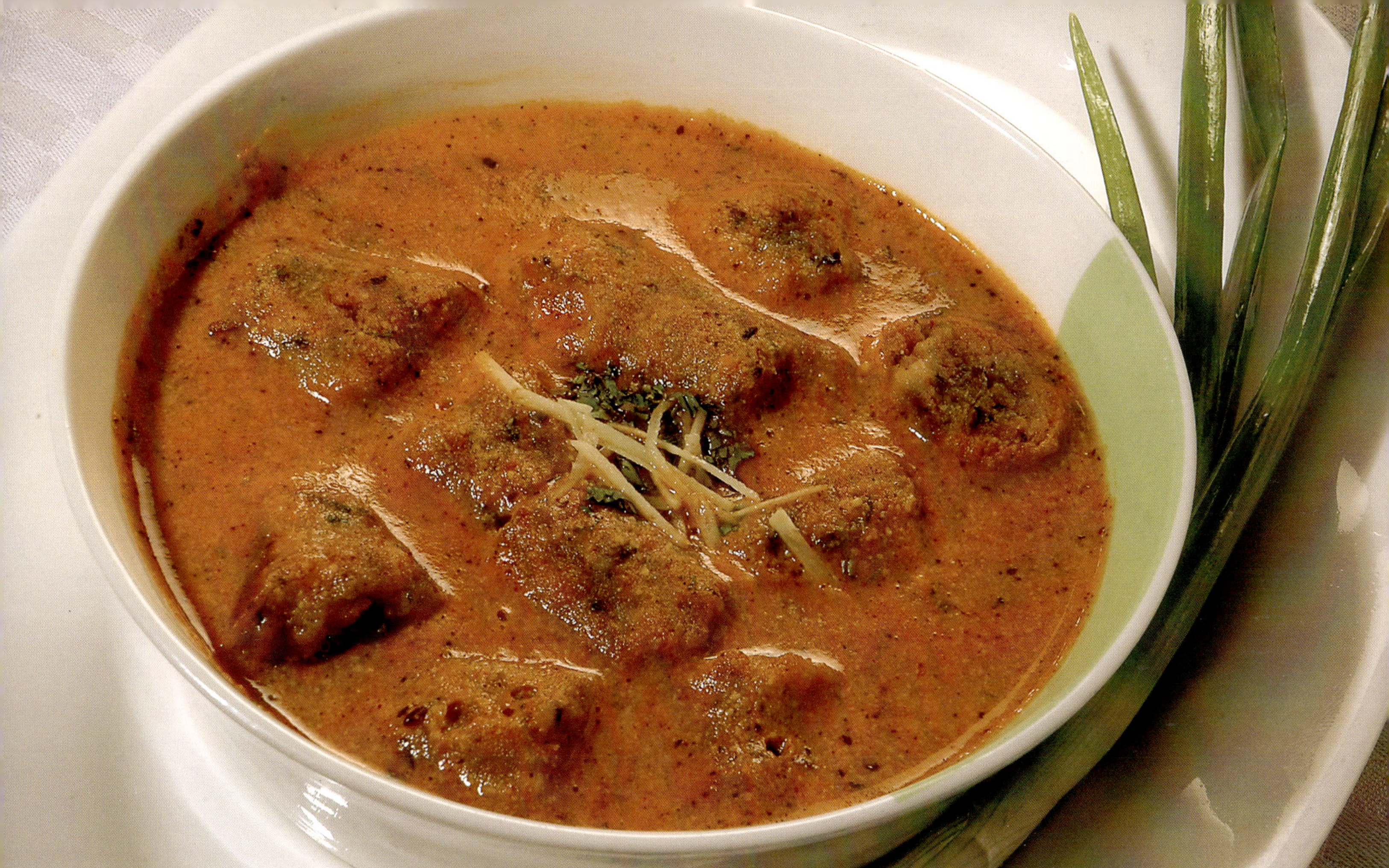

whisk to mix well. Heat *ghee* in a frying pan, add cumin and fenugreek seeds, stirring over medium heat until the seeds begin to pop.

- Add asafoetida, and stir until it puffs up. Remove from heat, and stir in the curd mixture. Stir-fry the fat till it leaves the sides. Add water (about 720 ml or 1/3 cup) and salt.
- Bring to a boil, reduce to low heat, add *gatta*, cover and simmer, stirring occasionally, until the gravy of thin sauce-like consistency is formed. Sprinkle green cardamom, clove, cinnamon and mace powder on top. Stir, sprinkle *kasoori methi*, stir and remove before adding the seasoning.

ABOVE
Bharwaan gatte *is a popular dish of the desert folk of Rajasthan where green vegetables are scarce*

AWADH

The Awadh region is the heart of the erstwhile United Provinces — the current-day Uttar Pradesh. Awadh (with Hyderabad in Deccan) became the custodian of the culinary tradition after the decline of the Mughal empire.

Although the institution of the Nawab of Awadh came to an end after 1857, it was the *taluqadaar*, rich landlords, who preserved the *nazaakat*, delicacy, and *nifaasat*, refinement, of the region. They lovingly preserved the legacy of Wajid Ali Shah, the legendary *bon vivant.* Wajid Ali was a lover of good things in life. He is credited with composition of lyrical *thumris* and is acknowledged as a generous patron of the Kathak dance form. The fun-loving prince mingled freely with his subjects and bridged the gap between the high and the folk culture. His court was considered a trendsetter in matters of taste, be it in cuisine or with costume. Melt-in-mouth *kebabs*, the *dum pukht* style of slow cooking and desserts like the silver-draped *shahi tukra* and *malai ki gilouri* testify to the significance attached to gastronomic delights during this period. Legend has it that the *dum pukht* style was adopted to facilitate the feeding of the vast labour force employed to build the majestic Bara Imambara at the time of a state-wide famine, by the compassionate Nawab Asaf-ud-Daulah.

As an intermediary between the local populace and the British, the *taluqdaar* often had to entertain on an opulent scale. The more lavish the spread the greater the access to the *Laat Sahib*, the Governor, and higher the reputation among the peer groups. It was not a question of the idle rich amusing themselves with affairs of the stomach; it was also a political necessity that dictated the delicacy and sumptuousness of the food.

It was during this period that the Mughal culinary repertoire came to be enriched with an infusion of countless indigenous streams. Chefs came from the adjoining *qasba* (townships) and villages, bringing with them their own recipes. Experimentation and innovation was encouraged. Talent and skill were amply rewarded and the acknowledged maestros were 'settled' in

RIGHT
Kebabs *require the deft touch of the cook of Awadh*

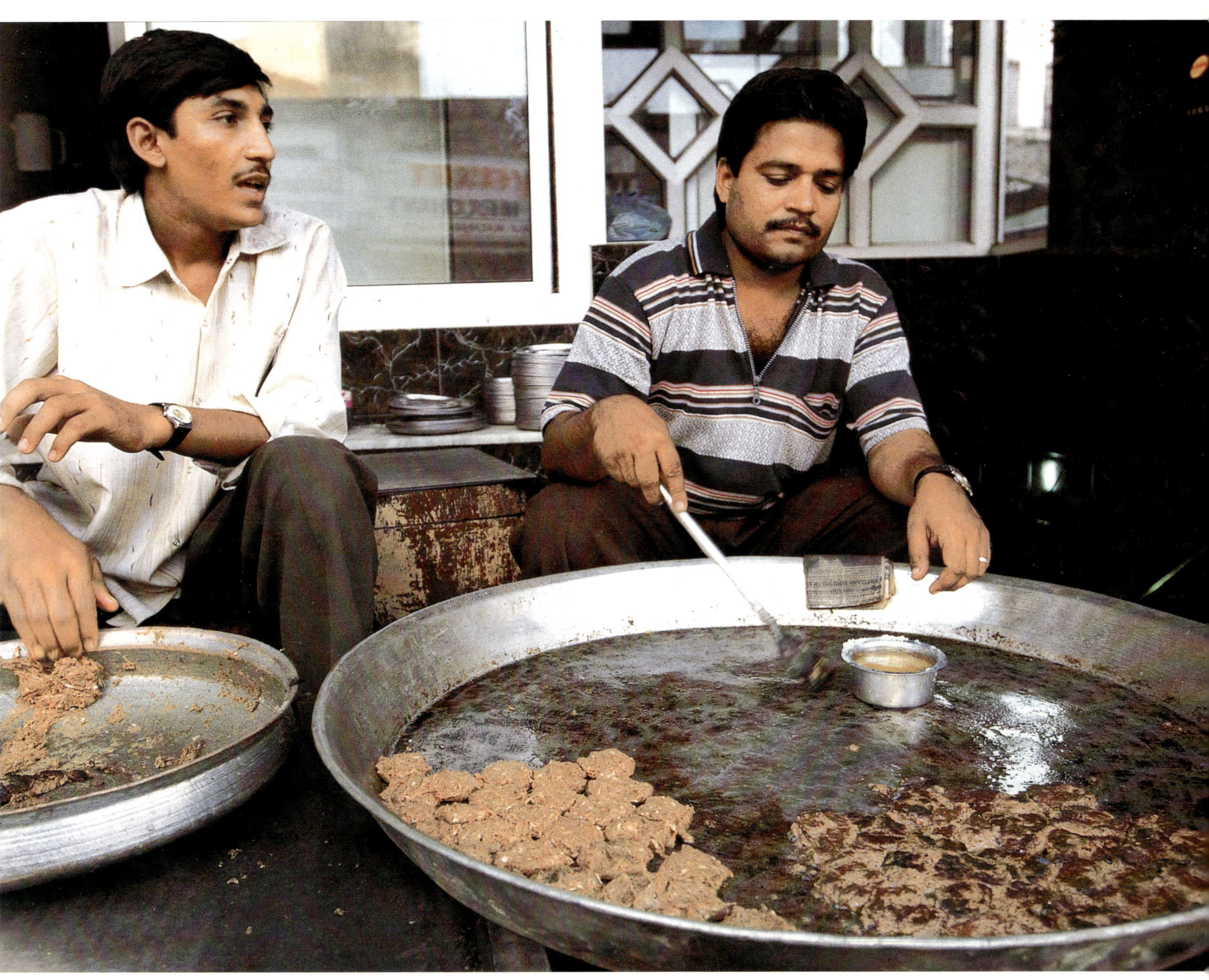

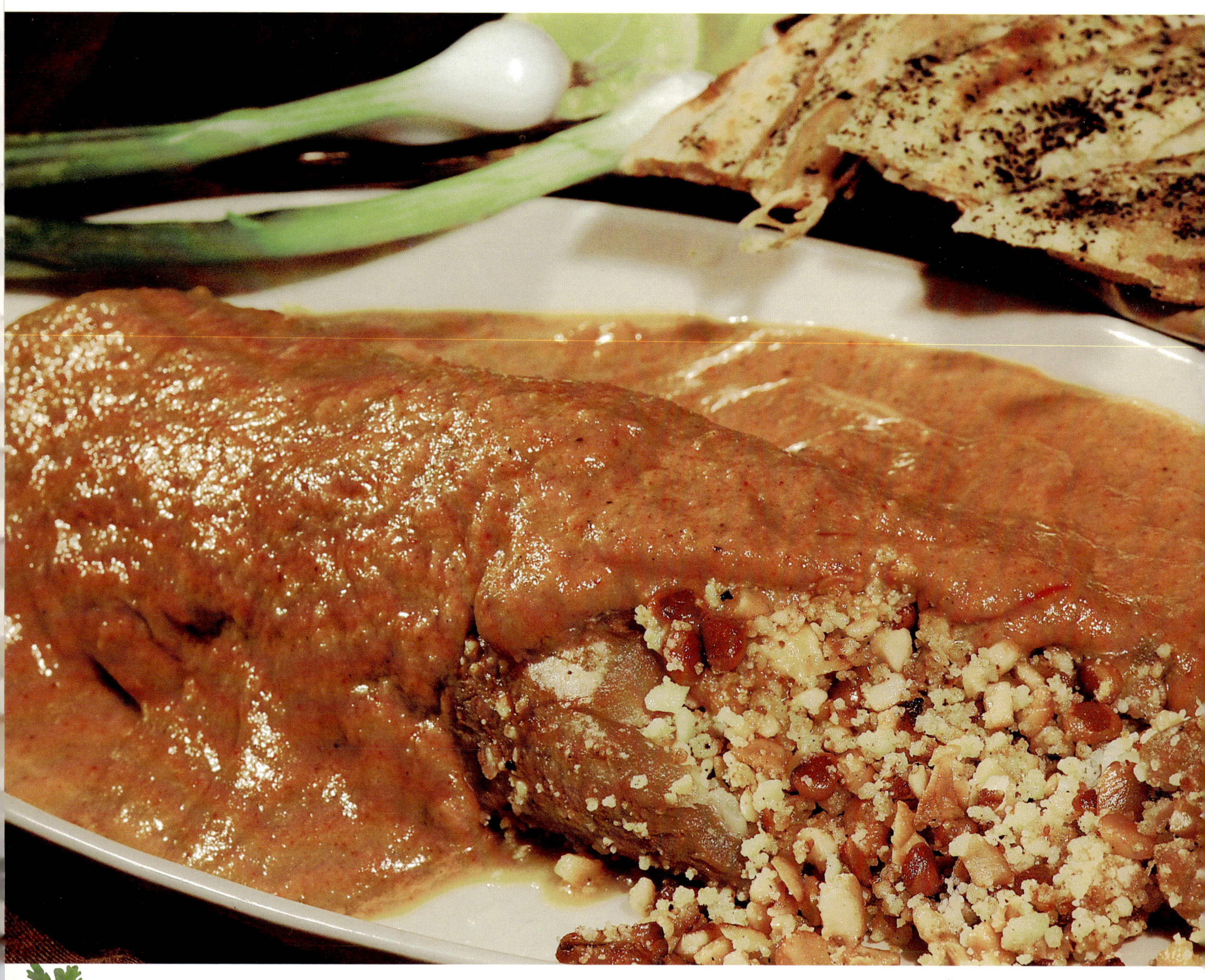

Lauki Mussallam

INGREDIENTS

500 gm bottle gourd
250 gm *khoya*
200 ml curd
2 tbsp poppy seeds paste
1 tbsp *chironji* paste
10 cashew nuts
2 onions (medium sized)
1 tsp chilli powder and *kewra* water
5 green cardamoms & cloves
1 blade of mace
100 gm *ghee*/oil
Salt to taste
A small sprig of green coriander
A pinch of saffron

METHOD

- Wash and peel the gourd. Remove the pith with a knife or with a thin and long blade. Prick the outside uniformly with a fork. Apply one tsp of salt all over and keep aside for 15 minutes.
- Fry the finely sliced onions to a golden brown and grind to a paste.
- Fry the cashew nuts and *chironji* separately in same *ghee* to a pink colour.
- Chop coarsely the cashew nuts and keep in a separate pan.
- Crumble the *khoya* and keep stirring till it turns to a pinkish hue. Mix the fried nuts in it and keep aside.
- Grind the cloves, cardamoms and mace to a paste. Lightly roast the poppy seeds on a griddle and grind to a paste using some of the curd.
- Pat the gourd dry and in the previously used *ghee* fry it evenly brown all over. Drain out the *ghee* and remove.
- Now add the *khoya* and salt with 2 tbsp of curd, blend well and stuff it inside the gourd. Mix the onion paste, poppy seed paste, *garam masala* paste and the saffron dissolved in *kewra* water with the curd.
- Also add the chilli powder and salt, blending it well.
- Grease a large flat pan, spread the curd mixture and the remainder of the *ghee* on it. Then cover with a lid and cook.
- Serve hot on a platter garnished with sprigs of coriander.
- Carve out round slices when serving.

LEFT
Lauki mussallam *is an indispensable part of the Lucknawi* dastarkhwaan

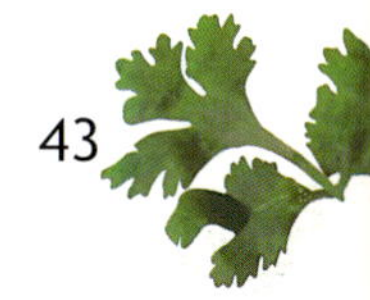

GOA AND COASTLINE

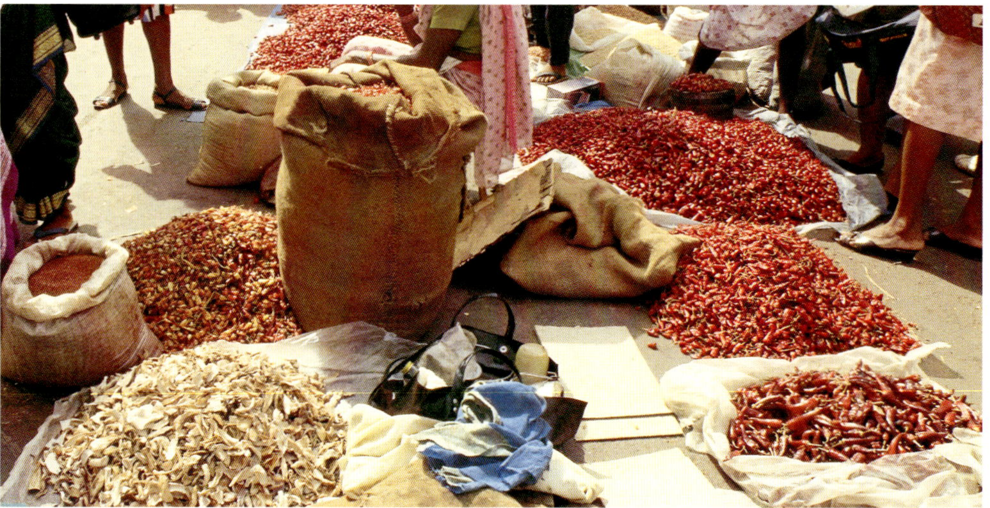

Vasco da Gama landed in Calicut in 1498 and claimed to have 'discovered' India. His successors moved northward to establish a foothold in Goa. Goa remained under the Portuguese rule for many centuries and this experience explains the imbibing and indigenising of alien tastes. The festive foods as well as the daily diet are more akin to the Western fare here than anywhere else. The culinary influence predates the arrival of the British and is very different from Anglo-Indian food. The churches, the carnival, the wayside taverns are an integral part of the foodscape of Goa.

ABOVE
Dry spices on sale in the weekly market of Goa

Goa Fish Curry

INGREDIENTS

750 gm fish (cut into pieces)
1 tsp lemon juice
1 tsp turmeric powder
8 red chillies (whole, soaked in 1 cup of water for 15 minutes)
1 cup coconut (grated)
3 tsp coriander seeds
2 onions (one chopped and one finely sliced)
1 tsp cumin seeds
1½ tsp garlic (chopped)
1½ tsp tamarind pulp

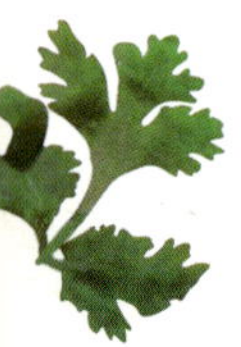

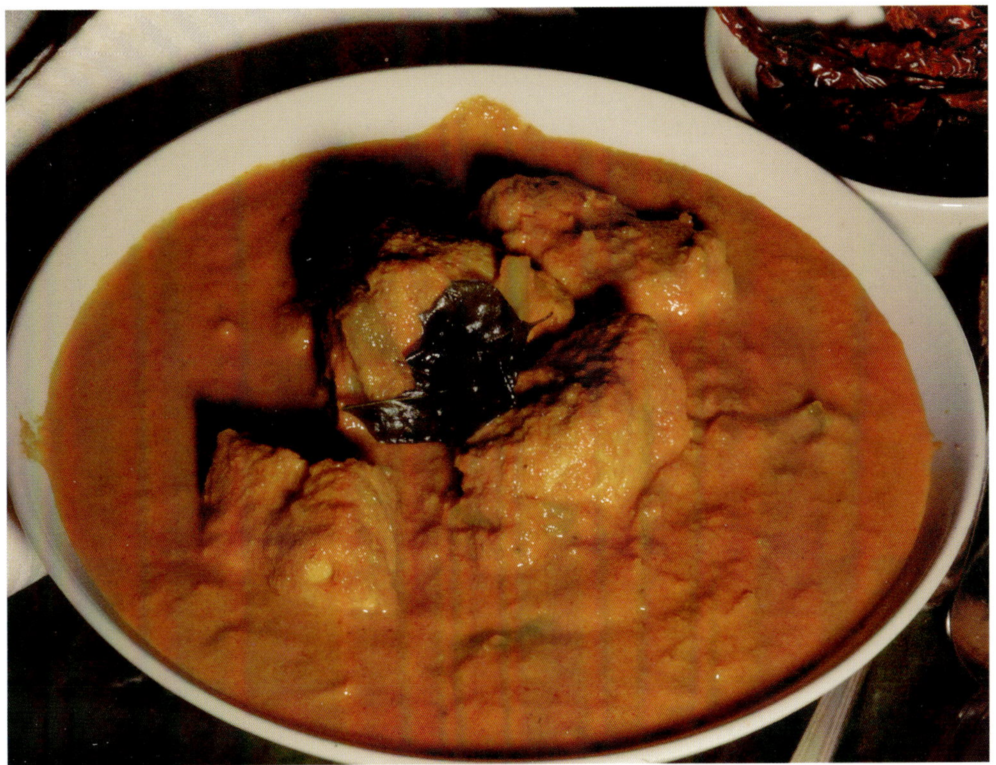

2 tbsp oil
1 tomato (purée)
3 green chillies (slit lengthways)
A few ladies fingers (optional)
Salt to taste

Method

- Prepare the marinade by mixing lemon juice with a pinch each of turmeric powder and salt.
- Rub this on the fish and keep aside for about 30 minutes.
- Grind chillies, coconut, coriander seeds, chopped onion, cumin seeds, the remaining turmeric powder, garlic, and 1 tsp tamarind pulp extract to obtain a smooth paste. Use a little of the water in which the red chillies were soaked.

ABOVE
Goan fish curry is immensely popular all along the western coast. The cuisine of Goa shows distinct Portuguese influence.

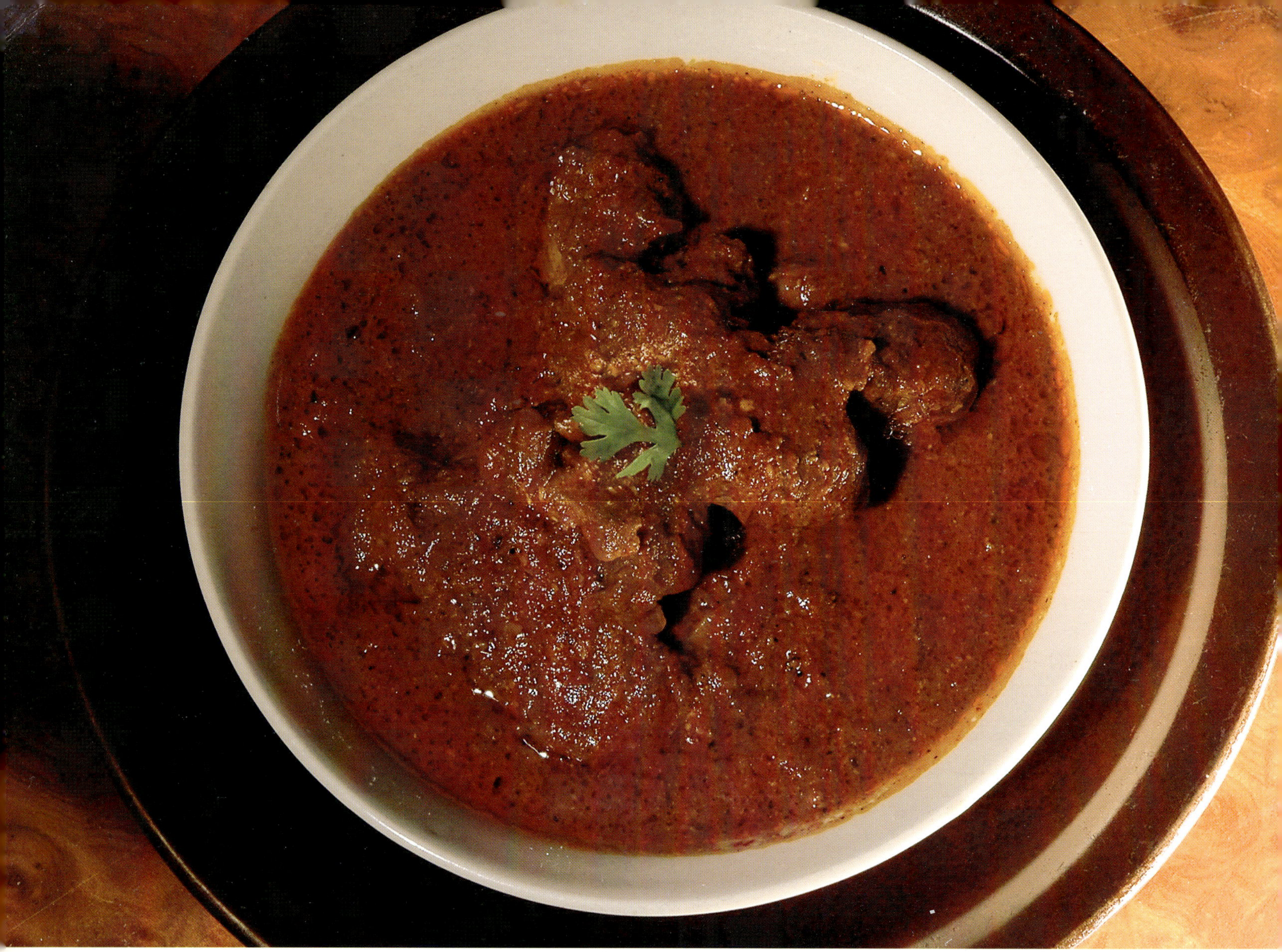

ABOVE
Chicken xacuti *is as exotic as its name suggests*

- Heat oil in a wide, shallow pan and stir fry onion for seven to eight minutes.
- Add the spice paste and cook on moderate heat for six or seven minutes, adding a little water if necessary. The paste should turn a golden brown.
- Add four cups of water when the oil begins to separate from the spices.

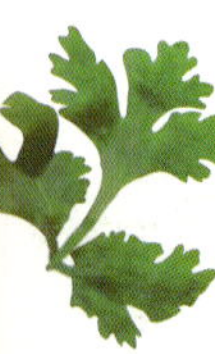

- Now add the tomato, green chillies, ladies fingers (optional), and salt to taste before cooking for about six minutes.
- Add the reserved tamarind water if desired, along with the fish and cook until done. Garnish with green coriander.

Chicken Xacuti

Ingredients

1 kg chicken (cut into10 pieces)

Spice Paste

10 dry red chillies (soaked in hot water for 10 minutes)
1 tbsp coriander powder
1½ tsp cumin seeds
1½ tsp fenugreek seeds
10 black peppercorns
3 tsp poppy seeds

½ cup coconut (finely grated)
¾ cup onions (sliced)
1 tsp turmeric powder
½ tsp green cardamom powder
½ tsp clove powder
½ tsp cinnamon powder
½ cup *ghee*/oil
2½ tsp garlic paste
2½ tsp ginger paste
½ cup lemon juice
Salt to taste

Method

- Prepare the spice paste by dry roasting each ingredient listed under this head separately until brown and grind together, adding water if required.
- Heat oil in a thick-bottomed pan. Add he spice paste with the garlic and ginger pastes, and stir-fry until th fat separates and rises to the surface.
- Place the chicken pieces in the pan with the salt. Stir to mix well. Cook until moisture evaporates.
- Add a cup of water, bring to boil and then reduce heat to allow it to simmer, by keeping the pan covered on low heat for about 10 minutes until the chicken is cooked.
- Sprinkle lemon juice and stir well.

to the vegetable. Cook the vegetables and drain them through a colander. Add the curd mixture and boil.

- Plantains, plantain stem, amaranth stem, chow-chow and ash gourd may be prepared into the *Aviyal* separately, using any one of these. *Moar kottu* is prepared in the same way with any vegetable. Season the preparation with mustard and black gram *dal* fried in coconut oil.

Pepper Prawns

Ingredients

24 prawns with tails
(about 24 or 1 kg)

Prawn Marinade

3 tbsp lemon juice
4 tsp garlic paste
2 tsp ginger paste
2 tsp black peppercorns (crushed)
Salt to taste

Spices

3 tbsp cooking oil
200 gm onions (chopped fine)
2 tsp garlic paste
1 tsp ginger paste
½ tsp coriander seeds (crushed)
¼ tsp red chilli powder
1 tbsp lemon juice
A generous pinch of black pepper powder (coarsely ground)
Salt to taste

Method

- Mix all the ingredients in a bowl, rub the prawns with the marinade and reserve in the boot itself for 15 minutes.
- Heat oil in a *kadhai*/wok, add onions and sauté over medium heat until translucent and glossy. Add the garlic and ginger paste, sauté until the onions are light golden.
- Add coriander and red chilli powders, stir-fry until the moisture evaporates. Then add the marinated prawns, increase to high heat and stir-fry for two minutes.
- Add ½ cup of water, stir; add lemon juice, salt and stir.
- Sprinkle the powdered spices, stir, remove from fire and add the seasoning.

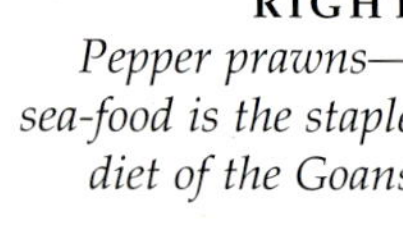

RIGHT
Pepper prawns—sea-food is the staple diet of the Goans

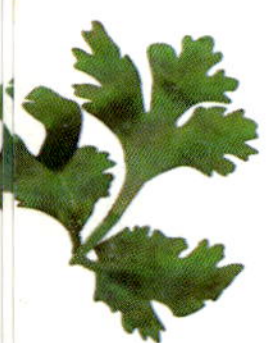

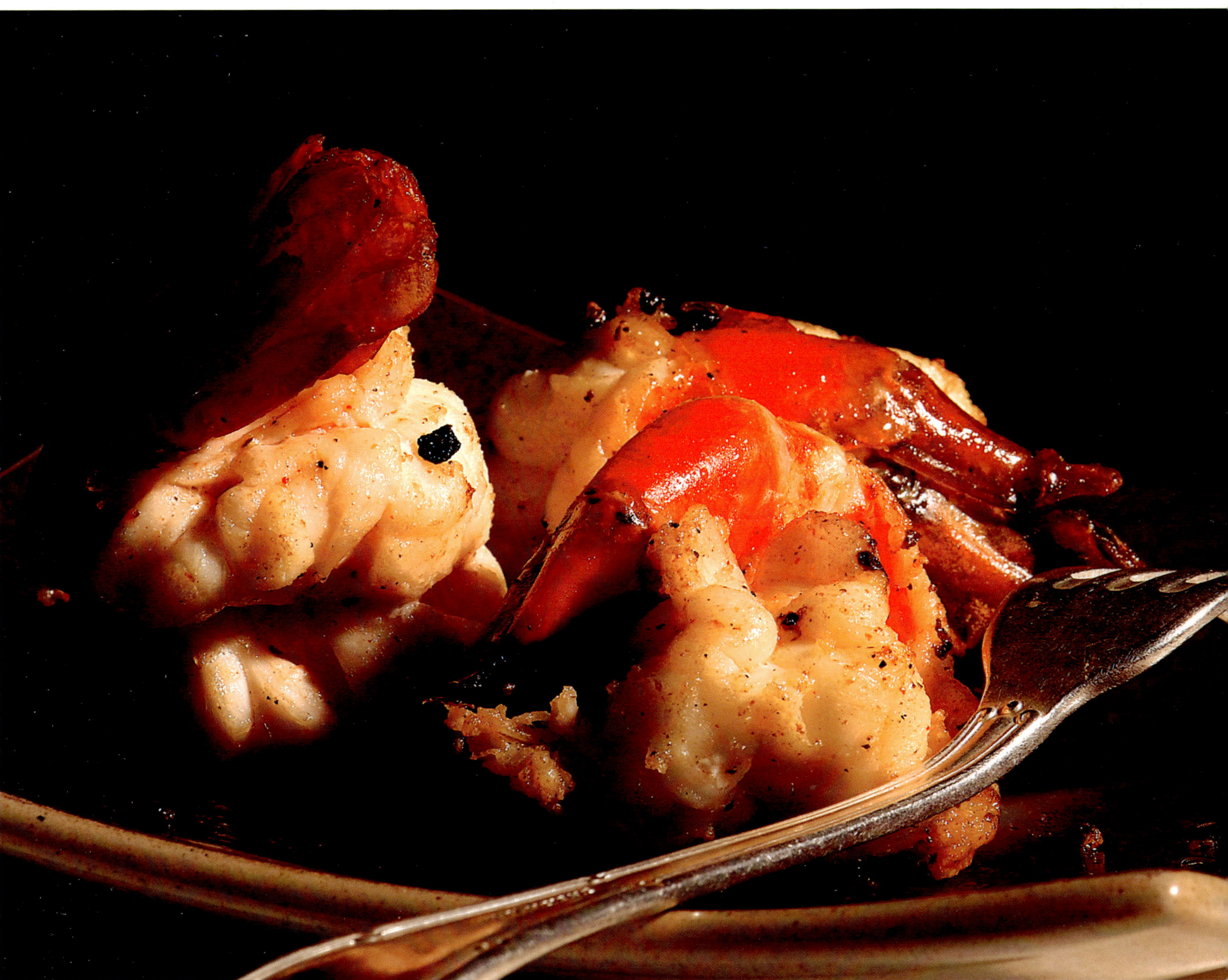

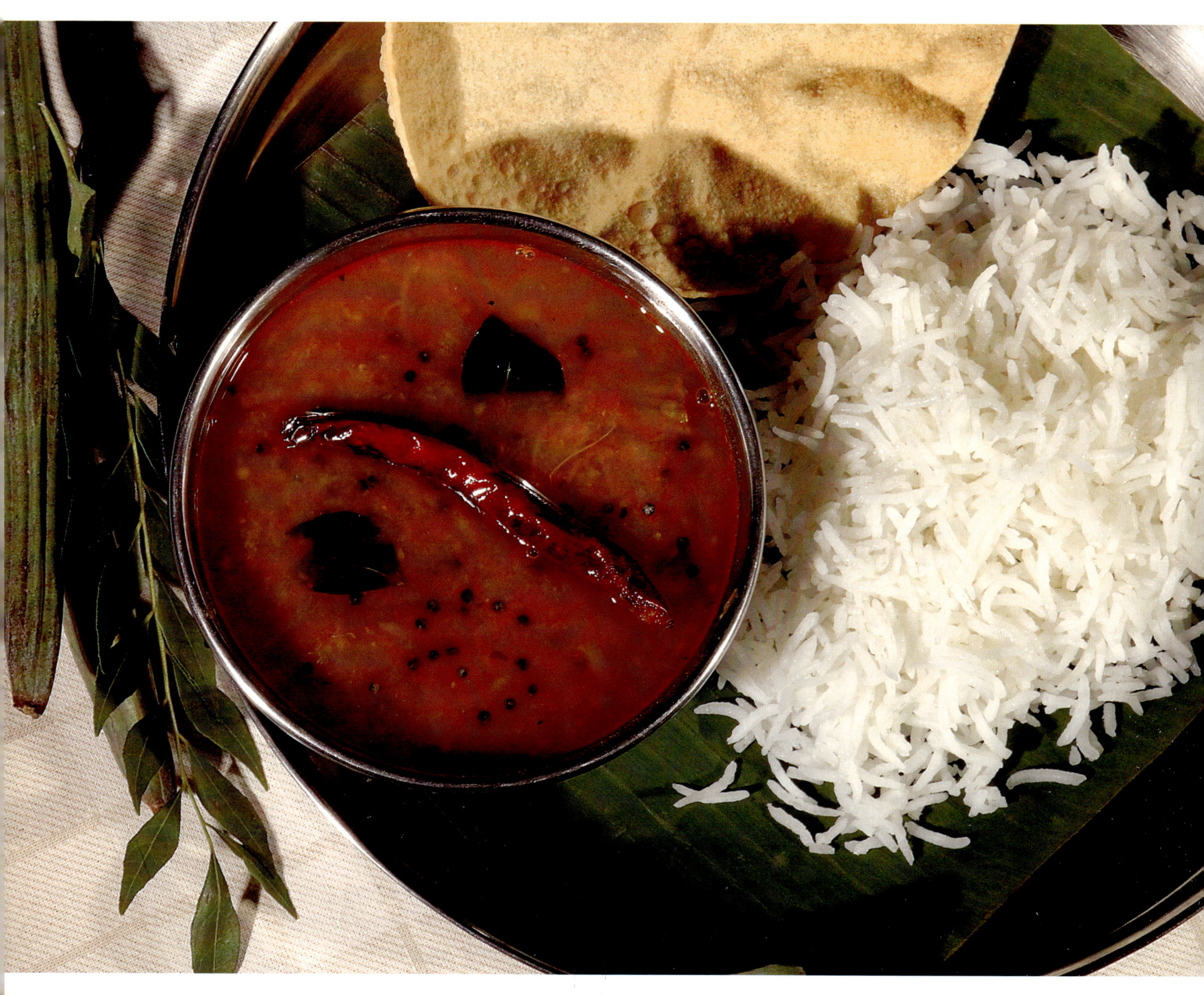

- Add 2 tsp of *sambar masala*, stir, add oil, and stir again. Reduce to very low heat and simmer, stirring occasionally, for about five minutes.
- Heat oil in a frying pan, add cumin, coriander, black sesame and mustard seeds along with the *urad dal*. Stir over medium heat until the seeds begin to pop. Then add curry leaves and asafoetida. Stir until the leaves stop spluttering and pour this over the simmering *sambar*.
- Now add tamarind pulp, stir, and reduce to low heat and simmer, stirring occasionally for 10-12 minutes. Add chopped coriander, stir, remove and pour the seasoning on top.

Vendakai Masala Pachchadi

INGREDIENTS

750 gm okra (washed, patted dry and cut into 1 inch pieces)
1 tsp cumin seeds
1 tsp mustard seeds
2 tbsp *urad dal*
3 whole red chillies
10 curry leaves
125 gm onions (chopped)
250 gm tomatoes (chopped)
1 tsp red chilli powder
½ tsp turmeric powder
1 tbsp coriander powder
75 gm coconut (grated)
2 tbsp cashew nuts
100 gm curd
Salt to taste
Groundnut oil to deep fry

METHOD

- Heat oil in a *kadahi* and deep-fry the okra over medium heat until crisp. Drain, keep aside and reserve the oil.
- Grind the coconuts and cashew nuts to a paste.
- Heat the reserved oil in a pan. Add cumin and mustard seeds, *urad dal*, whole red chillies and curry leaves. Stir-fry over medium heat until the seeds begin to splutter.
- Add onions and stir-fry until golden brown. Then add tomatoes, stir, and add red chilli, turmeric and coriander powders with salt. Stir-fry until the fat leaves the *masala*.

LEFT
A plate of rice, pappadam *and* sambar *is as popular in the north as it is in the south*

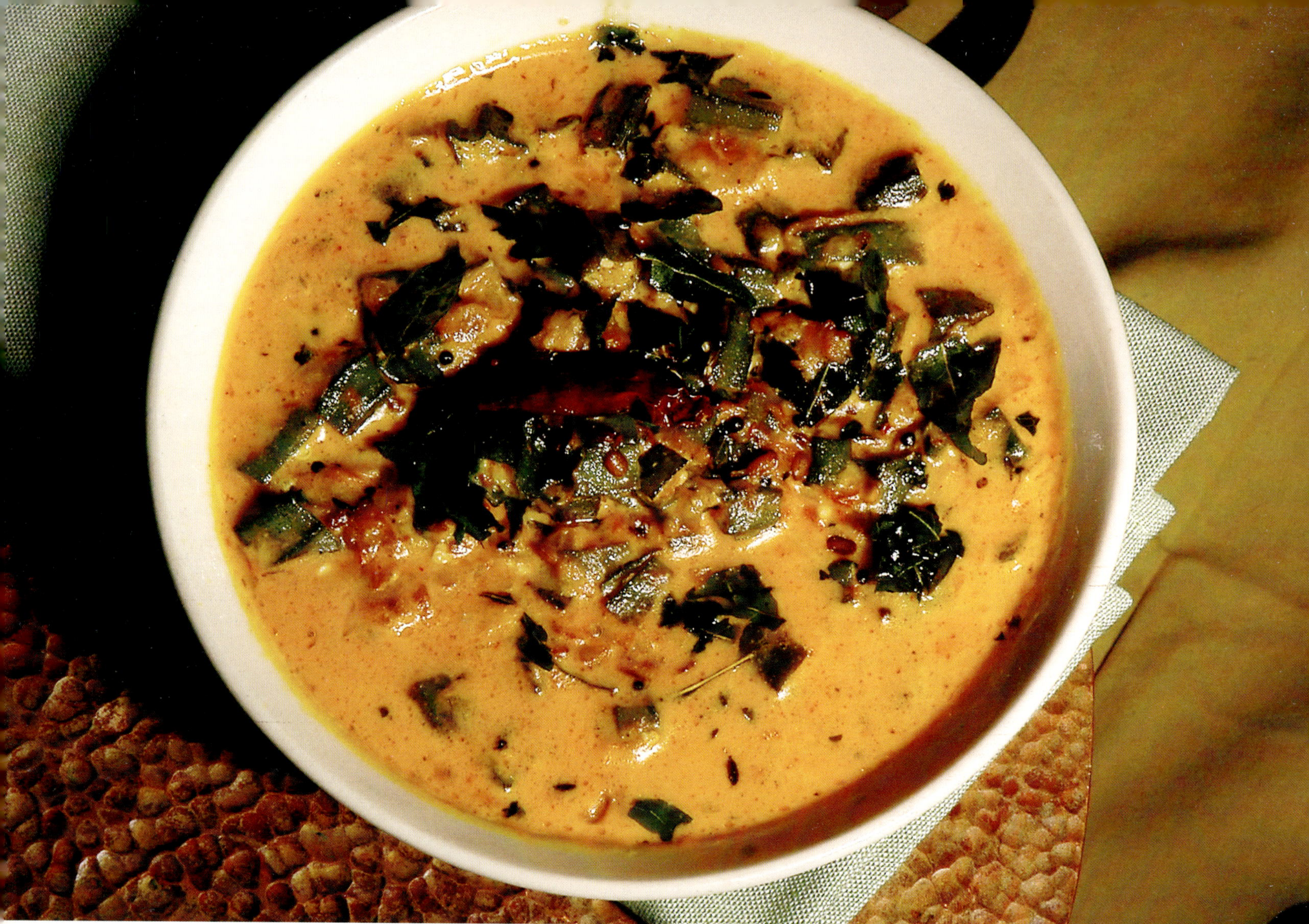

ABOVE
Vendakai masala pachchadi *is particularly relished with rice in the south*

- Reduce to low heat, add the coconut paste and fry for two minutes more.
- Remove the pan, add curd, stir and add water.
- Return to heat and bring to a boil. Now add the deep fried okra and simmer until covered with the gravy. Pour the seasoning over it.

HYDERABAD

The emphasis on elegance and subtlety coupled with a spirit of innovation are an integral part of food in Hyderabad, reminding us of Awadh. Here the Qutub Shahi and Asaf Jahi dynasties rekindled the fabulous legends of Golconda. It was in this historic city that north met south and the twain were never the same again. It is recognised as a domain of gracious living, courtly manners, tasteful cuisine and exquisite craftsmanship.

Who has not heard of the Nizam, Mir Osman Ali, the most exalted among the Indian princes, who was the only one to be accorded a 21-gun salute by the British? He may have been better known for his fabled jewels — at one time he was reckoned to be the richest man in the world — and accounts of the opulence of court life in his capital, Hyderabad, are, if anything, awe-inspiring. The gems, alas, have gone. What hasn't is the food. Hyderabd's food is as legendary as the sparkling diamonds of Golconda of yore.

Hyderabad escaped, as did much of the south, the political upheavals experienced by the other parts of the country. Tranquillity combined with wealth encouraged the princes and nobility to pursue a life of leisure without any distraction. Generous patronage allowed the culinary arts to blossom. Legend has it that the Asaf Jahi dynasty spent more time on matters culinary than on strategy or diplomacy.

It is hardly surprising that the Deccan boasts of, arguably, the most exotic cuisine in the land. Look at the rich influences from within — Mughal, Konkan, Maratha and Tamilian, and from without — Arab (Hyderabad was at one time the world's biggest market for Basra pearls and the Yemenis came to the city as tax-collectors for the Nizam), Persian, Turkish (the Nizams preferred to choose their brides from Turkey), Afghan and Turko-Afghan.

The key flavouring agents of Hyderabadi food are coconut, tamarind, peanuts and sesame seeds. The key spice is chilli, which is used in abundance and the reason for the sobriquet 'dynamite food'.

Hyderabadi Dum ki Biryani

Ingredients

250 gm rice (washed and drained)
500 gm leg of kid/lamb (*dasti*, shoulder, cut into chunks and pieces from the breast)
3 tbsp rose water
1 tbsp lemon juice
2 inch piece of ginger (chopped)
3-4 green chillies (chopped)
1/3 cup mint (chopped)
1/4 cup coriander (chopped)
4 tsp fried onions (sliced)
2 tsp saffron (crush threads with pestle, soak in lukewarm milk and then make a paste)
2 tbsp milk
1 1/2 tbsp *ghee*/clarified butter
Salt to taste

Aromatic Potli (Pouch)

5-6 green cardamoms (pounded)
5-6 cloves (pounded)

Spices for Meat

70 gm *ghee*/clarified butter
1/2 cup onions (sliced)
5 tsp garlic paste (strained)
15 gm ginger paste (strained)
5 green cardamoms
3 cloves, 2 sticks of cinnamon (1 inch long) and 2 bay leaves
1/2 cup curd (whisked)
1 tsp yellow chilli powder
2 tbsp lemon juice
1/4 cup cream
2/3 tsp green cardamom powder
1/3 tsp mace powder
1 drop *ittar*/rose essence
Salt to taste

Method

- Place the ingredients for the *potli* in a mortar and pound with a pestle to break the spices.
- Fold them in a piece of muslin cloth and tie with a string.
- Whisk the curd with yellow chillies.
- Boil 6 cups of water in a pan, add the *potli* with salt and stir. Then add rice and bring to boil.
- Add rose ersence and lemon juice, and continue to boil, stirring occasionally, until rice is nine-tenths cooked. Drain and discard the *potli*. Keep the rice aside.

RIGHT
Dum ki biryani, *the signature delicacy—a rich and aromatic dish—from Hyderabad is indispensable on most festive/celebratory menus*

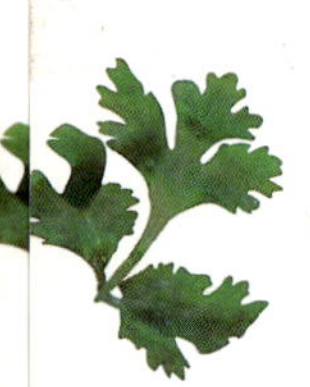

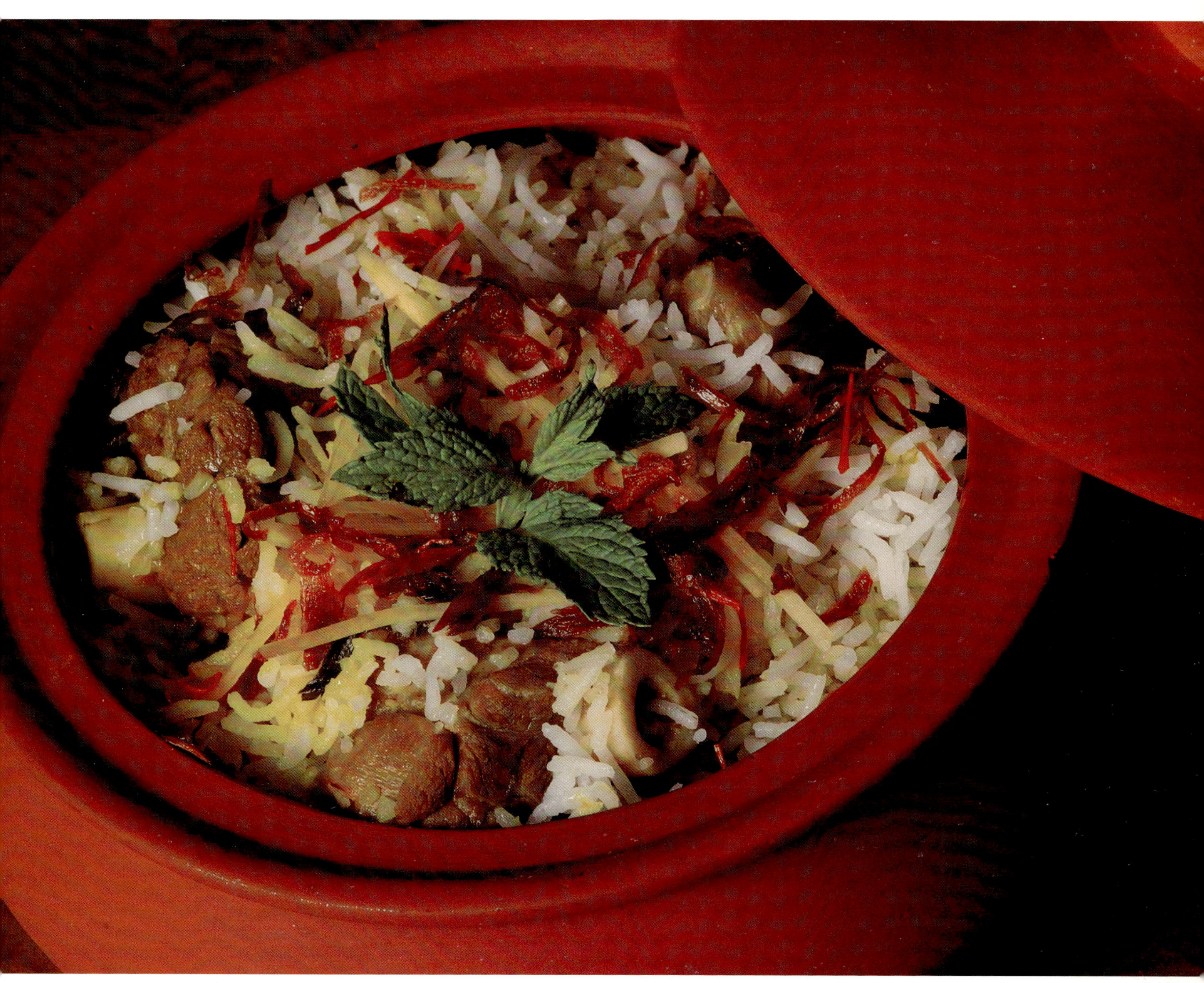

- Heat *ghee* in a pan, add cardamom, cloves, cinnamon and bay leaves while stirring over medium heat until the cardamom changes colour. Add onions, stirring until golden brown. Add garlic and ginger pastes, stirring for about 30 seconds.
- Add the mutton and stir for about two minutes.
- Add salt, stir, reduce to low heat, cover and cook, stirring occasionally for about 20 minutes (add water, if necessary). Uncover and stir-fry until the liquid evaporates.
- Remove the pan from heat, stir in the curd mixture, and return the pan to heat. Stir for about one minute, cover and simmer, stirring occasionally, until three-fourths of the liquid evaporates. Uncover and simmer, until the liquid evaporates and fat leaves the sides.
- Now add 2 cups of water and bring to boil, cover and simmer until the meat is almost cooked.
- Remove meat and squeeze the gravy through a fine muslin piece into a separate pan.
- Sprinkle lemon juice, stir, add cream, while stirring. Add the seasoning and reserve a quarter to be used during assembling.
- Return the meat to the remaining gravy, arranging it in the middle of the pan. Add mace and cardamom powders, stir and keep aside.
- Return the pan with meat to the flame. Sprinkle half ginger, green chillies, mint, coriander, fried onions and saffron.
- Arrange half of the partially cooked rice around the meat and sprinkle the remaining ginger, green chillies, mint, coriander, fried onions and saffron. Cover with the remaining rice, and sprinkle the reserved gravy.
- Pour on *ghee*, bring to boil and remove. Cover with a lid and seal with a lump of dough.
- Keep the sealed pan on *dum* in a pre-heated oven (350°F) for 15-20 minutes.

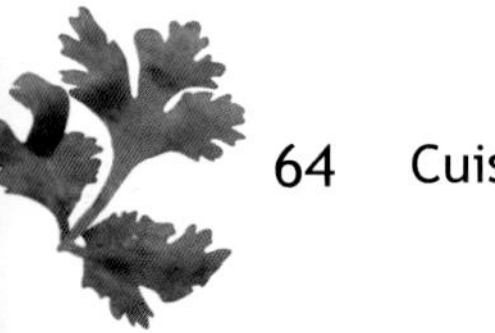

BENGAL

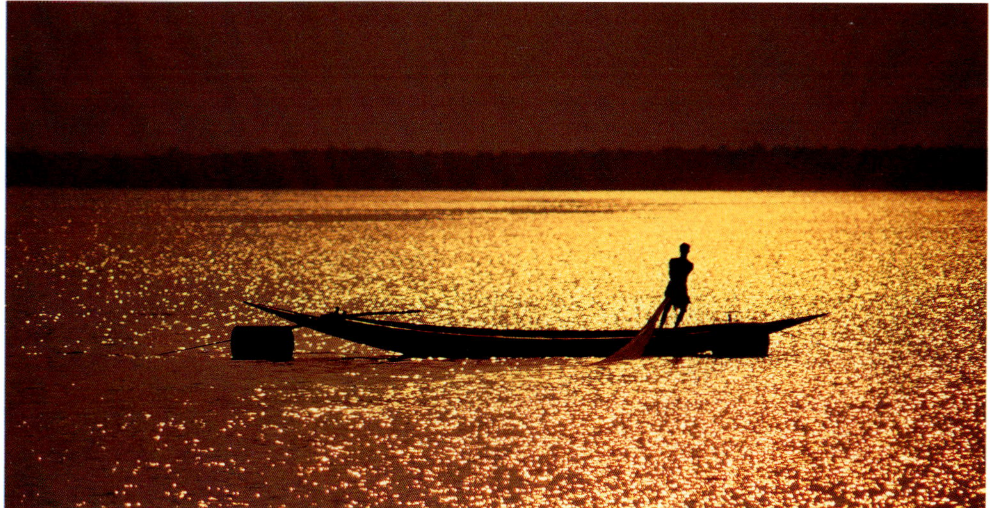

Bengal is synonymous with a matchless variety of delicate sweetmeats and irresistible fish curries. What is not very well known outside this many splendoured tract of land is that this is just the beginning of the state's delicious temptations. Food in Bengal follows more often than not the cycle of seasons, lays great emphasis on course-wise service and has always been open to stimulating influences from without. Nor are the vegetarian dishes neglected or overlooked — *shukto, ghonto, tok, begun bhaja, alur dom, alu potol, kamalanebu* with *kopi* are just a few of the perennial favourites.

Bengali cooking shows a marked preference for mustard, be it used as a paste or oil as the cooking medium. This style is not averse to use of a pinch of sugar in many of its recipes and has a distinct *garam masala* with strong regional identity, the *panch phoren.*

The Mughal *paratha,* the mince-filled *alu chop*, the *mocha* cutlet, the *kathi kebab* were all created in response to external influences — tastes introduced by immigrants, as by Wajid Ali Shah of Awadh or before him by the family of Tipu Sultan of Mysore. Calcutta served for generations as the capital of

ABOVE
A fisherman on the Arabian Sea hauling in his catch in the fishing net

British colonial administration and even after the pride of place was given to Delhi, it continued to be a bustling centre of commerce. This was indeed the 'city of joy' for those who had the means to enjoy. The province was in the vanguard of Western education, its residents seldom inhibited in adopting and adapting 'foreign' mores in costume and cuisine.

A sizeable Chinese population has helped Calcutta evolve an indigenous genre of Chinese cooking that can hold its own against the Hong Kong, Singapore or American versions.

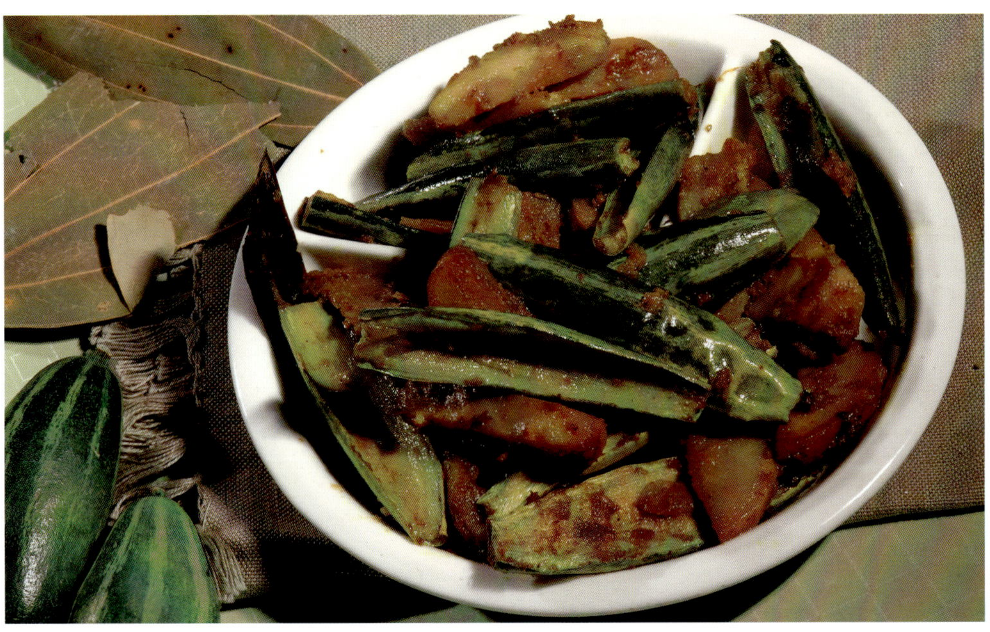

ABOVE
Alu potol *is a very popular Bengali dish made of fried potatoes and striped gourd*

Alu Potol

Ingredients

500 gm *parwal* (striped gourd), (tender, small and dark green ones)
150 gm potatoes (medium, washed, peeled and sliced lengthwise, to keep in water till used)
1 tsp garlic-ginger paste
1 tsp coriander powder
½ tsp turmeric
1 bay leaf
2-3 cloves
2 green cardamoms

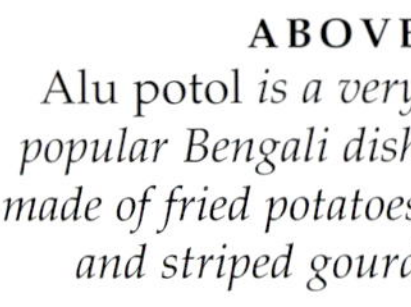

¼ cup refined oil
Salt to taste
A pinch of sugar (optional)
A small pinch of red chillies

METHOD

- Scrape the *parwal* and quarter-slice lengthwise. Keep aside in water.
- Heat oil in a pan and put the bay leaf in it. When it changes colour, add cloves and green cardamoms. After 30 seconds, add the garlic-ginger paste and stir-fry briskly. Sprinkle a little water to avoid burning the paste and then put in the spice powders dissolved in one tbsp of water.
- Add potato slices, while stir-frying for a couple of minutes.
- Then add the *parwal* pieces. Mix well, add 1½ cup of warm water, cover the pan and cook on low or medium heat till the potatoes are done.

Doi Machh

INGREDIENTS

1 kg white fish cut into cubes
½ cup mustard oil
1 cup curd (whisked)
Salt to taste

FOR MARINADE

1 cup onion (ground to a paste)
3 tsp ginger (ground to a paste)
10 cloves of garlic (ground to a paste)
1½ tsp cumin powder
2½ tsp chilli powder
½ tsp turmeric powder

METHOD

- Mix the ingredients for the marinade, add fish and let it marinate for an hour.
- Heat mustard oil in a wok till the oil smokes. Remove from heat and let it cool. Return to heat.
- Add fish and fry till golden brown.
- Add 10 tbsp of water, the curd and salt. Stir and simmer until the fish is tender. There should be some gravy left. Serve with rice.

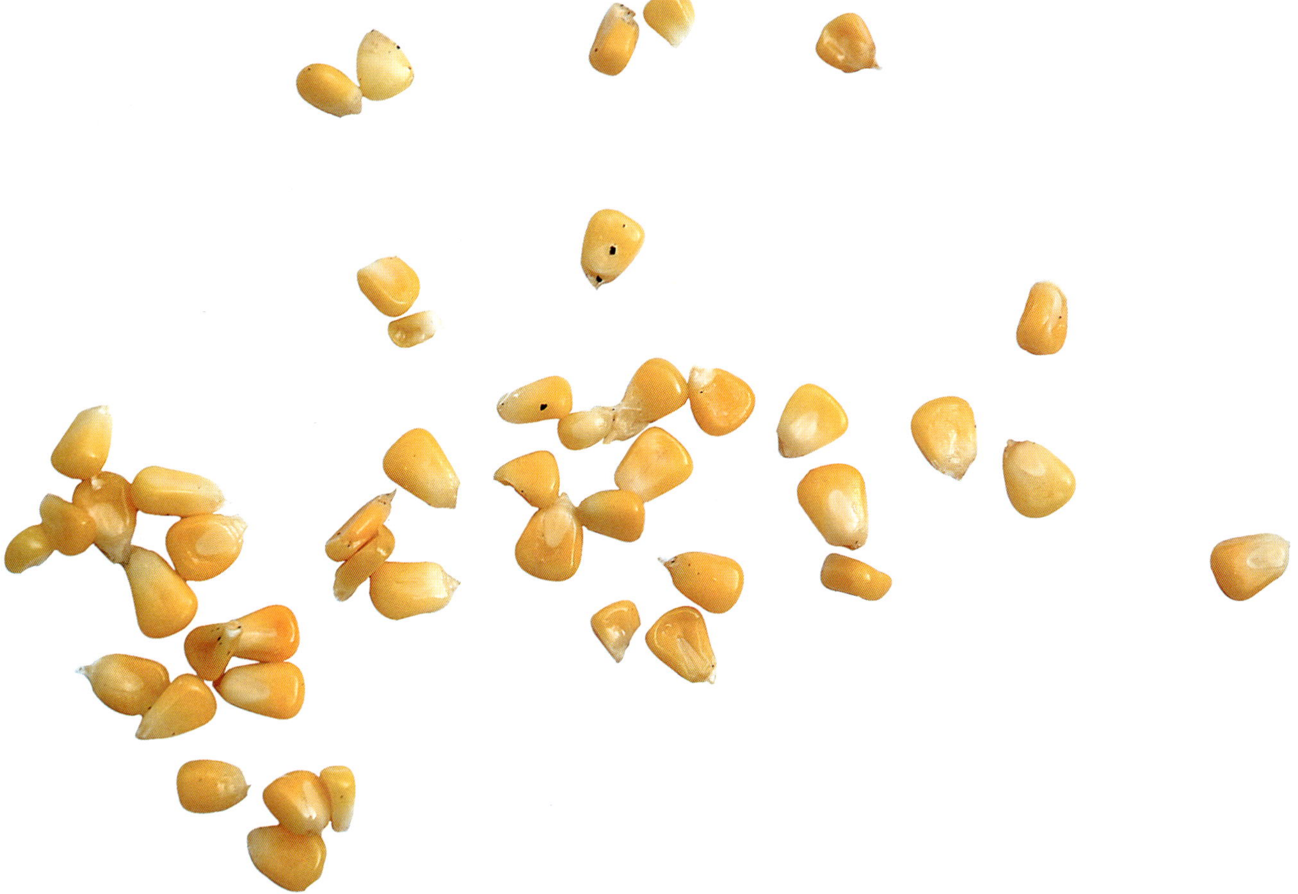

3 | Fusion During the Raj

The British came to the Indies with imperial ambitions but were seduced by the temptations of the sub-continent. They had to work hard, play hard and eat well. Many acquired a taste for local delicacies, married local women and made India their home. Thus were born the children of the Raj.

The Anglo-Indian encounter resulted in a unique intermingling of diverse flavours and cooking techniques, which spawned an unusually rich cuisine — that of the Anglo-Indians. Kipling, notwithstanding, East and West did meet at the dining table.

These culinary innovations were not confined to big cities. They were evident in *mofussil* towns, far-flung cantonments and railway colonies. What eventually came to be known as Anglo-Indian cuisine is in fact still 'preserved' in places like Chakladarpur, Bareilly, Ooty, Kharagpur, Hosur, Dehradun and many more.

Contrary to popular belief, their food is not bland 'Anglo', but spicy Indian. Their hospitality is unmatched, and their zest for life, incomparable. A traditional Anglo-Indian Sunday lunch, for example, is *bad word curry and yellow rice*. It is, actually, a *kofta* curry and rice. The *kofta* refers to meatballs. When the 'meat' was left out of the word, it became the 'bad word'. Or, for example, inability of some of them to pronounce the word 'capon' gave rise to 'captain'.

It is *déjà vu* for every Indian when they encounter Anglo-Indian food. Bengalis, Tamilians, Malayalees, Kannadigas, Punjabis and all the other lip-smacking Indians are quick to claim that this is 'our food'. What a tribute to a community that incorporated the best of the sub-continent to create a generic Indian cuisine.

The Europeans introduced many new crops into this region — tea, coffee and tobacco, vegetables like tomato, potato and corn and fruits like apple. In course of time, many have become more Indian than anything else. Darjeeling tea has long been relegated to the background, i.e. its 'mother', the Chinese tea. It is considered the champagne of teas. India is reckoned amongst the top producers of fruits and vegetables in the world. The spices that drew the Europeans to this land continue to be valuable foreign-exchange earners. Agro-industries and food processing provide large-scale employment. Familiarity with foreign taste has allowed Indians to cater to an ever-increasing fruit market. Popularity of ethnic Indian food is on the rise and one may well speculate that global taste in the next millennium will have a predominantly Indian flavour.

As the nation opens its 'doors and windows' to the world outside, it is no longer afraid of being 'swept off its feet by gusts of alien winds'.

On the contrary, Indian food is flourishing across the planet. As far as Britain is concerned, the Raj roles have been reversed. Curry waves rule Britannica. The British tourist authority is now promoting Bombay Brasserie, Chutney Mary, Red Fort and other Indian eateries as 'destination' restaurants in England.

The biggest gain in the last 50 years has been the 'creation' of a pan-Indian cuisine. The Punjabi *dhaba* and the southern *udippi* are now ubiquitous, and have wrought a revolution in taste. A *tandoori* chicken is enjoyed as much in Kerala as a *dosa* in Ladakh. Bengal's sweetmeats, arguably the best in the land, have found purveyors of equal skills in Rajasthan, while the Rajasthani *bhujia* (salted deep-fried snack) is creating waves in Bengal. There's more than just taste involved here. This fusion reflects independent India's coming of age. It would be no exaggeration to state that if Lata Mangeshkar tunefully integrated the country, this pan-Indian food has tastefully brought together the rich and the diverse populace of this vast land.

Indian food served in homes had, and still has, a perfect and subtle balance. Indians eat sequentially, a course after a harmonious course, to indulge all the senses. Take south India, for example. The meal commences — and this is auspicious — with a milk-based *paayasam*. The *paayasam* is followed by vegetables — fried or simmered in gravy, usually both. The next course is steamed rice, the staple, with *desi ghee* or clarified butter, *appam* or *poppadom* and *sambar*, the ubiquitous lentil delicacy. Then comes *rassam*, served with more steamed rice and *varuval* — fried chips made from raw bananas, tapioca, yam or potatoes. Next in the sequence is *thaeer saadam* or curd rice, which 'cools' the system and is served with pickle. The dessert is some more *paayasam* or sweets liks Mysore *paak* or a *laddoo*.

Similarly, the Bengalis, the Maharashtrians, the Kashmiris, in fact most Indians eat sequentially, but not when it comes to entertaining — at home or in a restaurant. With such a rich legacy of fine formal dining, it is surprising that our restaurants have not yet learnt to serve our delicacies in a balanced manner.

With the world shrinking and everyone's appetite for new culinary experiences growing, the Indian genius for creative cooking is on the threshold of a grand renaissance.

FOODLORE

KHUBANI KA MEETHA

Khubani or apricots are a fruit believed to have been imported into the sub-continent by the Central Asians. Babur, about whom every schoolboy continues to be taught, pined for the fruit of his native land, Fargana, as he led dangerous military campaigns on the hot Indian plains. Little did this founder of the grand dynasty know that the prune with the velvety skin had reached his beloved homeland from China via India. Historians speculate that this transit took place when Alexander the Great's entourage was transporting it to Europe in the 4th century BC. So enamoured were the ancient Greeks with the apricots that they gave them the name, the 'golden egg of the sun'.

Well, Indian apricots continue to be tasty, luscious with a tang and delightfully sweet with just a hint of sourness and a refreshing aroma. Orchards in Kashmir, Himachal Pradesh and Uttaranchal produce the best and regional partisanship renders a fair decision on which region produces the best impossible. There is the *badami* variety where the 'almond' yielded by the pit stone is difficult to distinguish from the real Mc Coy and the *morpankh,* the larger platter specimen that resembles the beautiful marks on the peacock feathers, is decidedly more fragrantly flavourful.

Apricots ripen earlier than peach, plum or pears, hence the name that shares etymological roots with precocious. The fruit has a short shelf-life and it is not surprising that most of us are acquainted with it as a dried fruit

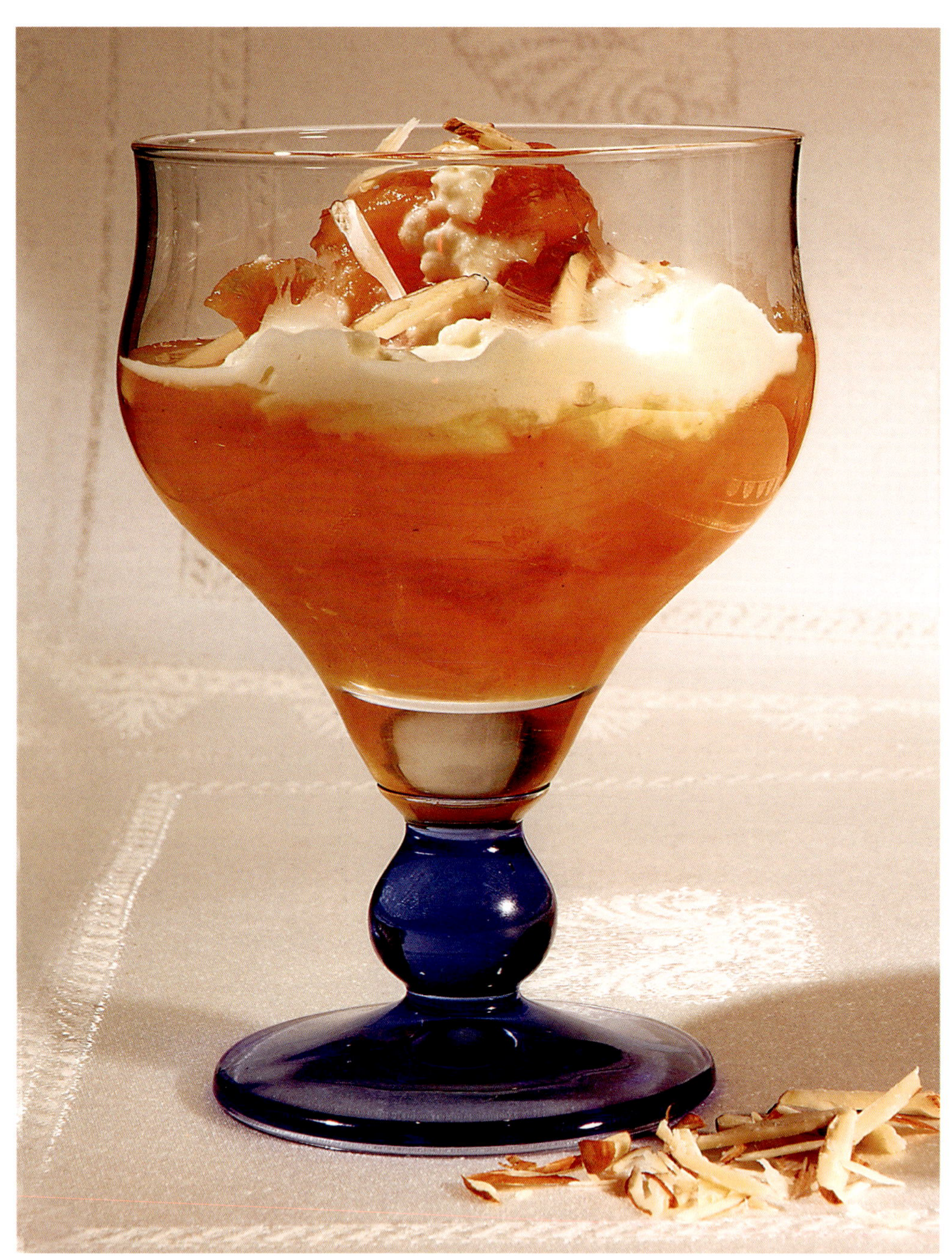

or in its incarnation as a preserve. Those who are a little squeamish about imbibing alcohol are perfectly happy to sip apricot brandy deluding themselves that it is a fruit-based innocent beverage and that the act does not entail any loss of innocence. *Khubani*, however, can be used, and *is* used, in some very interesting non-vegetarian delicacies. The Kashmiris make unusual meatballs that are shaped like dried apricots and packed with raisins to ensure a fruity taste. The Parsis call dried apricots *jardaloo* and use them lovingly with chicken in a sweet-and-sour dish that is indeed sublimated by the fruit.

However, our own favourite continues to be the sublime apricot-based dessert that may be served, if you are lucky, in Hyderabad. More often than not, it is the *double ka meetha* that one encounters or, if a more elaborate banquet is being hosted, *gille firdaus* or *badam ki jaali* relegates this simple yet elegant sweet to the background. This dessert should not be confused with stewed or poached apricots dunked in sugar syrup. Just remember that the dried apricots have a much higher calorific value than the fresh fruit and although the temptation is always strong to reach for the second, one should not yield without some resistance. Do not insult the *khubani ka meetha* by topping it with a slab of ice cream; it should be married only with clotted cream.

Apricot

Ingredients

1 kg dried apricot
150 gm sugar
250 gm fresh cream

Method

- Soak apricots overnight in just enough water to cover them. Add half the sugar to the apricots while soaking.
- Next morning, boil the apricots in the same water till tender.
- Remove the seeds. Sieve till only the fibre remains in the strainer.

LEFT
Khubani ka meetha—*a dessert prepared with fresh apricots and topped with cream and milk to gratify a sweet tooth*

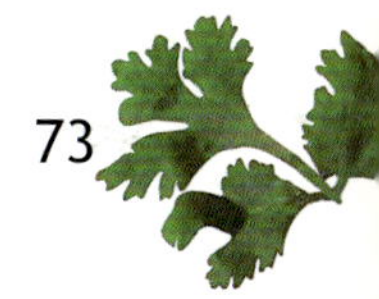

- Add a little water and the remaining sugar and cook on medium heat till the desired consistency is obtained.
- Crack open the apricot seeds and remove the kernel. Blanch the kernel and remove the skin.
- Garnish the dish with these apricot kernels. Serve with *malai* (clotted cream).

SAMOSA

Samosa is arguably the most enduring of Indian snacks. It is a staple fare in canteens and hostel messes and is ubiquitous on railway-station platforms. The *samosa,* like a *tikki,* can be conveniently packed between two slices of bread or a split bun to create a filling for a sandwich. A friend insists that the *samosa* is an inspiration for the *vilayati samosa* — a patty! It is inevitably encountered in *chaat* shops across the land and there are some *halwais* who take greater pride in their *samosa* than anything else. Lokenath in Allahabad has built an enviable reputation on the strength of his *ghee ke samose dal ki pithi wale.* These *samosas* have a fairly long shelf-life.

In many small towns, the *samosa-jalebi* combo is what is synonymous with *jalapan* (refreshment) or *kaleva*, breakfast or tiffin on the go, or a semi-formal celebration. Even the diehard hypochondriac reaches for a *samosa* without any fear as the boiling oil has temperature that he believes is capable of destroying the toughest of the microbes. Countless corner kiosks thrive on their daily sale to loyal patrons of this tea-time delight. In Bengal, it is called *singhara,* perhaps due to their triangular shape recalling the water chestnut. And, then there are the mini cocktail *samosas* — dainty 'li'll' things — the perfect finger-food to tuck in before imbibing the fiery stuff.

Samosa is basically a savoury stuffed with potatoes, peas, or minced meat. And, this is just for the starters — you are limited only by your fancy — mushrooms, chopped eggs and pickled olives, sprouts, cheese and what have you can be used as a filling. It is quite common to enrich the *samosa* with

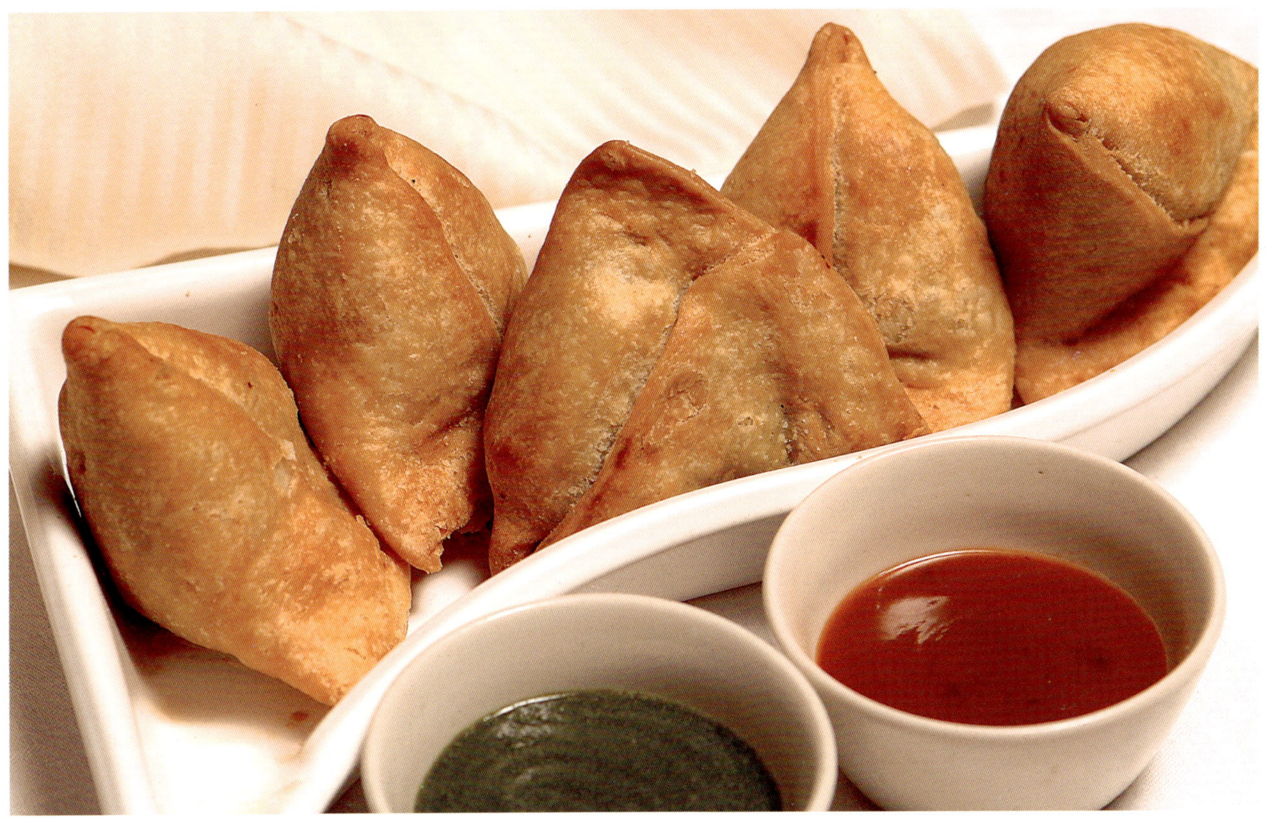

dried fruits like raisins and nuts like the cashew. (There *are* sweet *samosas* too like the *lavanglatika*.) Some health-conscious people are apprehensive about the deep fried *samosa* but may we remind them that a well-made *samosa* does not ooze oil; on the contrary, these are bone dry. If you are still scared, yield to the baked version of the sinful temptation.

A *samosa* that is truly memorable does not have a thick crust; instead, it envelopes the filling in a thin drape — one can even imagine that it is translucent! It is comparable to a perfect dumpling. The casing can be pepped up by sprinkling the dough with *ajwain* (caraway) or *kalonji* (nigella) seeds.

ABOVE
Samosa *is a popular snack eaten separately or as a filling in a sandwich*

Amir Khusro, our own renaissance man, mentions *samosa* in his description of delicacies enjoyed by the princes and nobles in the Sultanate period *circa* 13th century. It was prepared, we are told, with meat, *ghee*, onions, etc. This testimony is cited in support of the thesis that *samosa* is a foreign import. However, others quote chapter and verse from ancient Sanskrit texts to dispute this. There did exist a delicacy called *samushak* that is virtually indistinguishable from the familiar stuff.

Samosa

INGREDIENTS

THE CASING

300 gm flour
Salt
Cooking oil, 60 ml

FILLING

Boil the mashed potatoes and peas spiced with powdered cumin, *anardana*, green chopped chillies or lightly sauted button mushrooms with mixed herbs or cooked minced meat mixed with chopped hard-boiled eggs or assorted sprouts with carrot juliennes and diced string beans.

METHOD

- Stir the flour with salt. Make a bay and pour the oil in it.
- Then, knead the dough reasonably hard, adding a little water if required.
- Roll out discs like a *poori,* cut into halves.
- Lightly oil your palms and shape the halves into a pouch by bringing the two sides of the crescent together. Place a little filling and seal the top after moistening the inner surface with water.
- Set aside and fry or bake in batches. Serve with chutney or any sauce of choice.

POPULAR DESSERTS

Shahi Tukrha

INGREDIENTS

350 gm *rabri* (unsweetened)
600 gm sugar
1 drop of rose water
½ tsp green cardamom powder
12 slice milk bread
2 litre milk
4 tsp almonds
2 tsp pistachio
2 tsp saffron
Silver leaves (*chandi-ka-varq)*
Groundnut oil to deep fry

METHOD

- *Rabari*: Add 100 gm of sugar while it is still warm and stir until dissolved. Add vetiver and stir.
- *Syrup*: Boil the remaining sugar with 300 ml of water to make a syrup of one-string consistency. Add cardamom powder and stir.
- *Bread*: Slice off the crust and trim the edges to make discs. Heat oil in a *kadahi* and deep fry over low heat until golden brown and crisp.
- *Milk*: Bring to a boil in a large, flat, thick-bottomed *handi*, remove and reserve 1 tbsp to dissolve saffron.
- *Tukrha*: Immerse the fried bread in the remaining milk, with the slices at least an inch apart. Return the *handi* to heat and simmer until the milk is absorbed, turning once in between with a spatula without breaking the bread. Remove from heat and pour on the warm syrup.
- *Nuts*: Blanch almonds and pistachio, cool, remove the skin and cut into slivers.
- *Saffron*: Dissolve in the reserved milk while it is still warm.
- *Assembling:* Arrange the soaked *tukrha* on a silver platter, spread *rabari* on top, garnish with nuts and sprinkle saffron.
- *To Serve*: Cover the *Shahi Tukrha* with *varq* and serve warm.

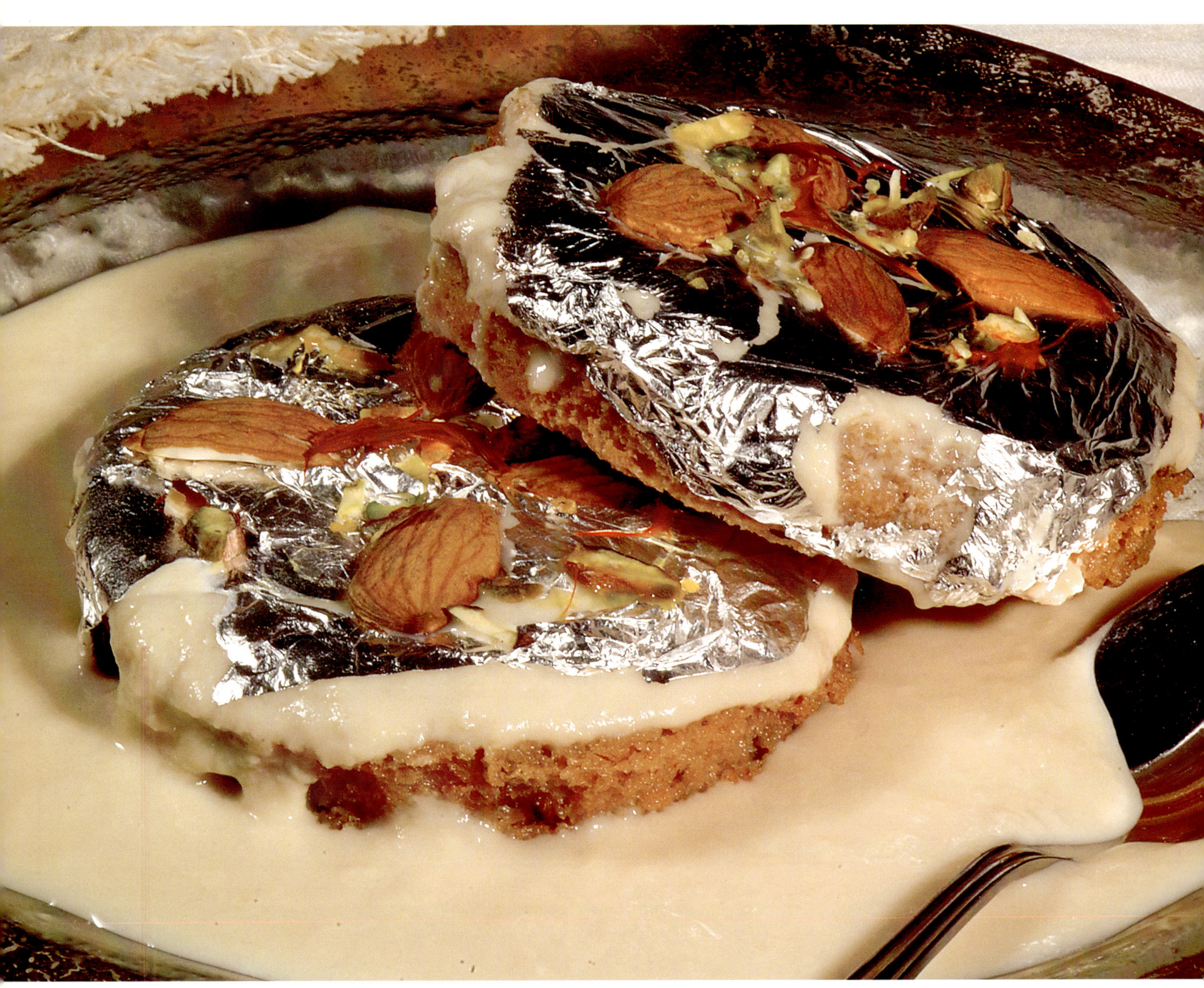

Kesari Kheer

INGREDIENTS

1.5 litres milk
75 gm Basmati rice
4 tsp *ghee*
125 gm sugar
1 tsp green cardamom powder
3 tbsp almonds
5 tsp raisins
2 tsp saffron
2 tbsp milk to dissolve saffron

METHOD

- *Rice*: Pick, wash in running water and soak for an hour before draining.
- *Almonds*: Blanch, cool, remove the skin and split.
- *Saffron*: Dissolve in warm milk.

COOKING

- Boil milk in a *handi* and remove.
- Heat *ghee* in a separate *handi*, add rice and fry until it begins to colour (about 45 minutes).
- Transfer the milk and bring to a boil, stirring constantly (to ensure that the rice does not stick). Reduce to low heat and simmer until the rice is cooked.
- Add sugar and continue to cook until reduced to a custard consistency. Now add the remaining ingredients, and stir for a minute.
- Remove to a silver bowl and serve hot.

BREADS

Sheermal

INGREDIENTS

1 kg whole wheat flour
3 cups *ghee* or white butter
2 cups milk
1 tsp cardamom powder
1 tsp salt
3 tbsp sugar
2 tsp yeast
4 tbsp screwpine flower water (*kewraha*)

LEFT
Shahi tukrha *decorated with* rabari *and nuts is the best way to end a meal*

METHOD

- In the milk add the yeast, screwpine flower, water, cardamom and sugar. Mix well and set aside.
- In an open tray, mix the flour with salt and *ghee*. Pour the milk mixture into the tray to make a dough of soft consistency and set aside for two hours.
- Now divide the dough into 24 equal-sized balls. Roll each ball with a rolling pin into a disc of 6-inch diameter. Prick the disc with a fork. Place the disc on a preheated griddle and cook on both sides till golden brown.
- Do the same for the rest of the dough balls.

Baqarkhani Roti

INGREDIENTS

4 cups flour
1 tsp baking powder
3 tsp sugar (powdered)
1 cup full cream milk
1 tsp fresh yeast water
4 cardamoms (powdered)
2 tbsp raisins
16-18 almonds (cut in slivers)
1 cup *ghee*
1 tbsp poppy seeds
Salt to taste

METHOD

- Sift flour with baking powder and salt. Add sugar and warm milk. Keep aside.
- Soak the yeast in ¼ cup lukewarm water and keep aside for about 30 minutes to rise.
- Mix flour with the yeast including the milk in which it has been soaked and knead well.
- Mix cardamom, raisins and almonds into the dough. Keep in a warm place for at least an hour.
- Add half the *ghee* and knead again. Divide the dough into a dozen equal parts and shape into balls. Keep aside for 30 minutes.

RIGHT
Baqarkhani roti *is a bread with a difference — it is sweet*

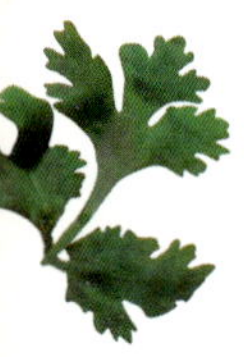

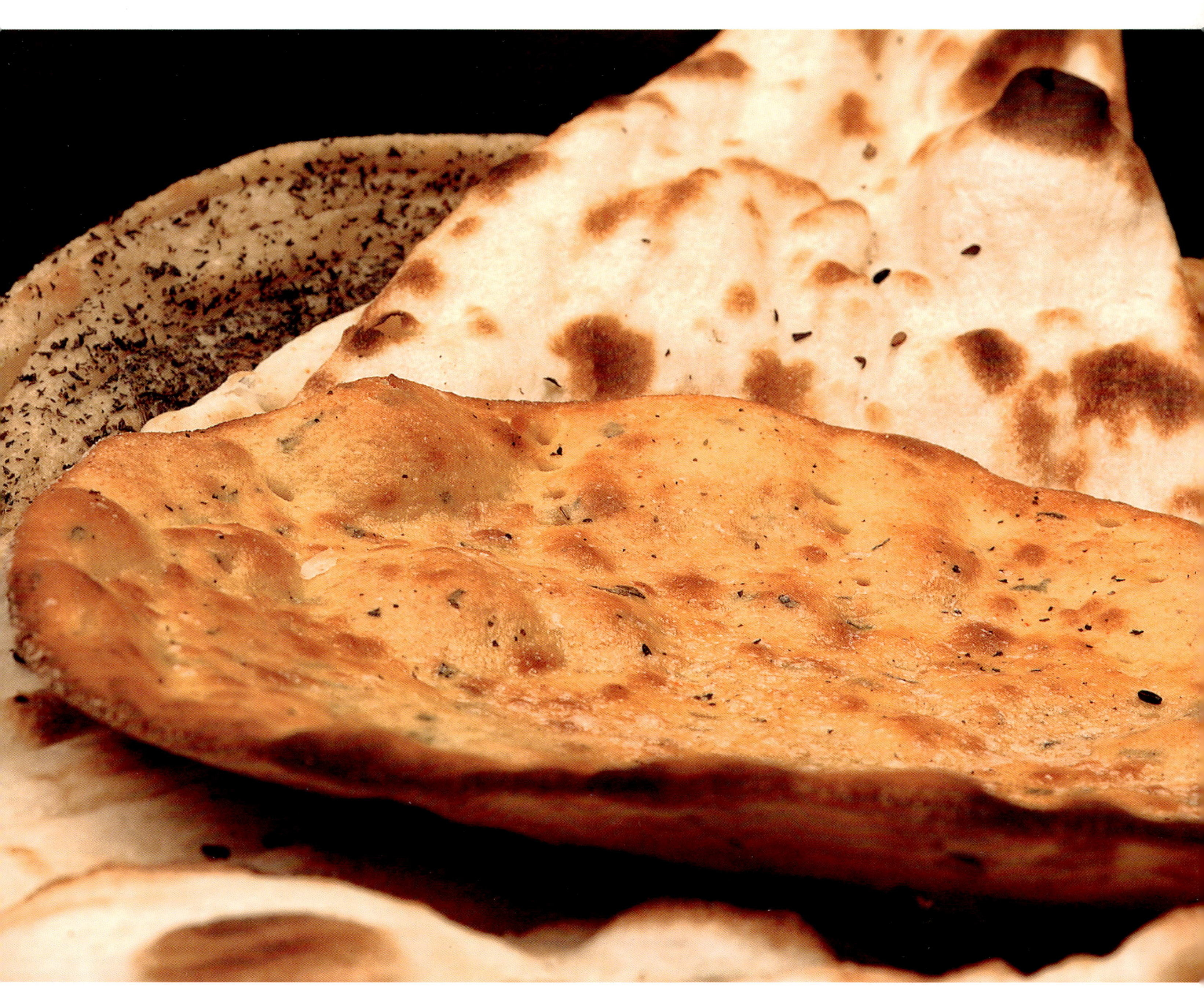

- Flatten the balls into patties of about 7-inch diameter and about one-eighth of an inch thick.
- Brush with *ghee* and fold each in four. Roll into balls again. Leave for 10 minutes. Repeat the entire process thrice.
- Sprinkle the poppy seeds over them. Bake in a preheated oven at 375°F for about seven to eight minutes.

Lachha Parantha

INGREDIENTS

3 cup *atta* (whole wheat flour)
3-4 tbsp *ghee*
¼ tsp salt

METHOD

- Mix the flour with *ghee* and salt. Add water and knead well to obtain a non-sticky dough. Keep aside for about an hour.

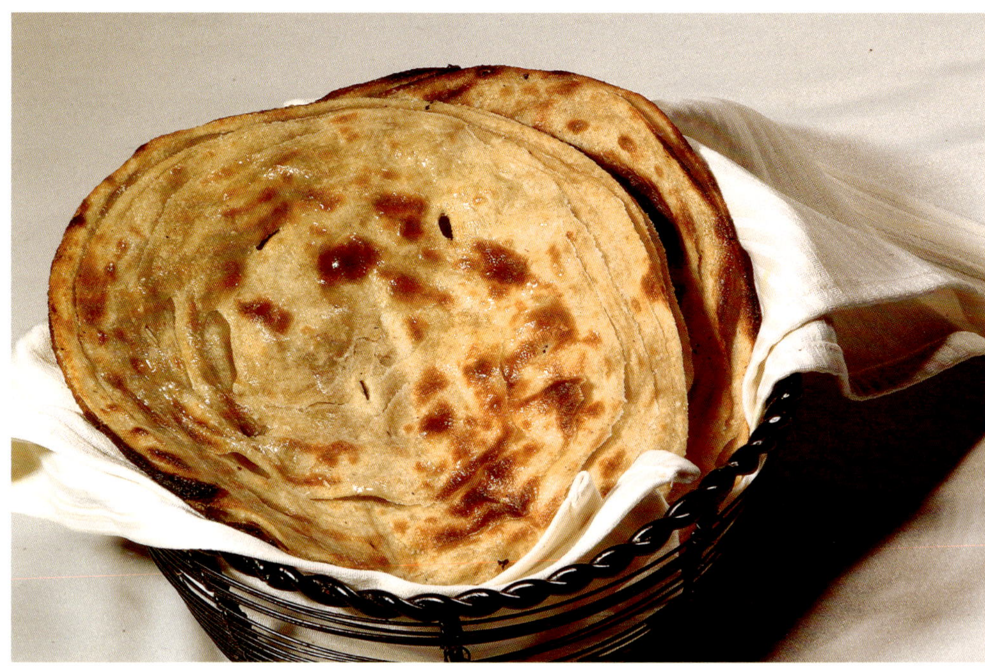

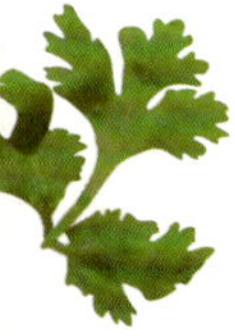

- Knead again and make six balls, each the size of a large onion. Roll out each to a disc of about 8-inch diameter. Spread 1 tsp *ghee* all over the disc and dust some flour over it.
- Now pleat the disc lengthwise into one collected strip. Twist this strip. Coil the strip to get a *pedha* (resembling a flattened ball, a bit like a coil of rope).
- Flatten this *pedha* between the palms of the hands or gently roll on the rolling board with the rolling pin, without applying too much pressure, to obtain a small, thick *parantha* of about 6-inch diameter.
- Cook in a *tandoor* after applying a little water on back of the *parantha.* Alternatively, it may be cooked on a hot *tawa* also. When using a *tawa,* first brown both the sides lightly on a hot griddle. Reduce the flame and then fry on low heat, applying *ghee* till rich brown (on both sides). Press the sides all over the *parantha* with a spoon while frying to ensure that the thick *parantha* gets evenly cooked.

Amritsari Kulcha

Ingredients

500 gm plain flour (*maida*)
½ cup clarified butter (*desi ghee*)
200 gm potatoes (peeled and grated)
175 gm cauliflower (washed and grated)
2 tbsp cottage cheese (grated)
2 tsp ginger (chopped)
1 tbsp coriander (fresh and chopped fine)
1 tsp coriander (seeds, broiled and crushed)
1 tbsp green chillies (deseeded and chopped)
¼ cup onion (chopped)
1 tsp black pepper powder
1 tsp dried pomegranate seed powder (*anardana*)
1 tsp cumin seeds
1 tsp cardamom seeds
1 tsp dried fenugreek leaves
1 tsp *garam masala*
Salt to taste

LEFT
Lachha parantha *can be eaten with pickles, if a vegetable curry is not available*

METHOD

- Mix all the ingredients except the salt, plain flour and clarified butter in a bowl and divide it into eight equal portions.
- Sieve the refined flour with salt in an open stainless steel platter (*paraat*).
- Pour some water in the sieved refined flour and start mixing till a soft dough is made. Keep this dough aside for about 30 minutes and cover with a moist cloth.
- Add half the clarified butter, knead again and cover and keep aside the dough for another 10 minutes.
- Now, make eight balls from the dough and put aside for about five minutes.
- Now, put the balls on a floured surface, one by one, and go on flattening with a rolling pin into round discs of about 4- or 5-inch diameter.
- Put some filling in the middle of each such round disc, enfold the filling and then seal the edges. Flatten the disc again with a rolling pin, taking care not to let the filling ooze out.
- For cooking, one can either use a *tandoor* or an oven. In a *tandoor*, place the flattened disc on a cushioned pad and stick inside a moderately warm *tandoor*. Let the disc bake for two to three minutes and then take it out with tongs. While using an oven, place the disc on a greased baking tray and let it bake for about 10 minutes. After removing the baked *kulcha*, apply clarified butter and serve hot.

Makkai ki Roti

INGREDIENTS

500 gm maize flour (*makkai ka atta*)
60 gm whole wheat flour (*atta*)
25 gm plain flour
100 ml butter
Salt to taste

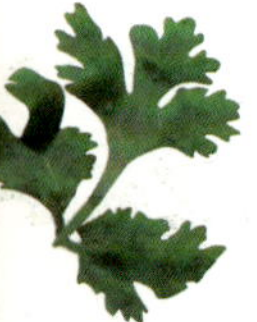

Method

- Sieve the maize flour, wheat flour (*atta*), plain flour and salt into a mixing bowl. Pour water in the flour and knead till a soft dough is made. Cover with a moist cloth and keep aside for about 30 minutes.
- Divide the dough into eight equal portions, make balls, dust with flour, cover and keep aside for about five minutes.
- Now, flatten each ball between the palms or alternatively roll with a rolling pin to make a round disc. Sprinkle flour to prevent it from sticking.
- Place the *roti* on a *gaddi* (cushioned pad) and stick it inside a moderately hot *tandoor* and bake for about two minutes. In the pre-heated oven, place *roti* on a grease baking tray and bake for about six minutes. Remove from the *tandoor*, apply *ghee* on each *roti* and serve with *sarson da saag*.

RAITA AND CHUTNEY

Makhane ka Raita

Ingredients

100 gm *makhane* (lotus seeds)
2 tbsp *chironji (priyala seeds)*
1 tbsp raisins
2 cup milk
½ cup cream
1 pinch sugar
50 gm *ghee*
½ kg curd
Salt to taste

Method

- Remove the hard black flakes from the *makhane* and boil in milk for eight minutes. Drain milk from *makhane.*
- Heat *ghee* and lightly fry *chironji*, raisins and keep aside. Now pass the curd and cream through a muslin cloth.
- Add salt and a pinch of sugar, *makhane, chironji* and raisins. Blend gently and serve chilled in a bowl.

Burrani

INGREDIENTS

250 gm curd
½ tsp pepper
Salt to taste

METHOD

- Sieve the curd through a fine muslin cloth or a fine sieve.
- Add salt and pepper and blend well.
- Serve in a bowl along with a *korma* and *pulao* dish.

Coconut Chutney

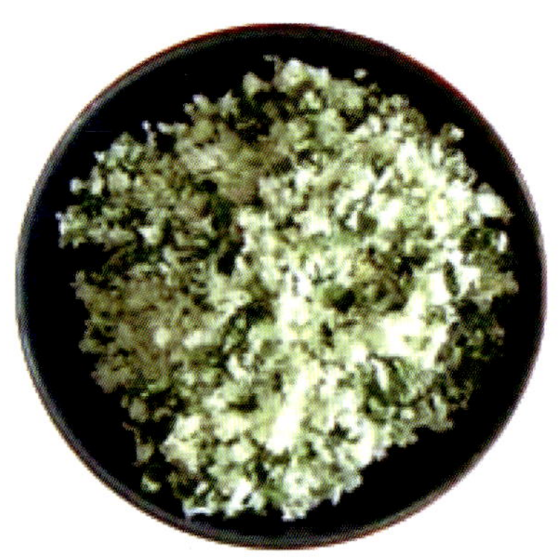

INGREDIENTS

2 cup scraped fresh coconut
2 pieces of green chillies
1 tbsp Bengal gram (soaked)
1 tbsp sugar or jaggery
1 tbsp tamarind pulp
1-inch piece of ginger
1 clove garlic (optional)
Salt to taste

FOR TEMPERING

2 tbsp oil
½ tsp mustard seeds
½ tsp white split gram
¼ tsp asafoetida
A few curry leaves

METHOD

- Grind all the ingredients together in a small grinder with a little water into a fine paste.
- Heat oil in a small vessel and add mustard seeds. When they splutter, add white split gram, asafoetida and curry leaves.
- Pour this over the prepared chutney and serve with south Indian snacks.

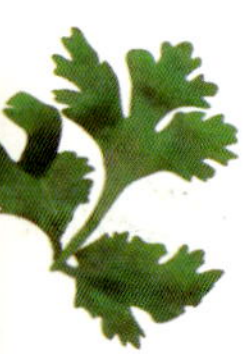

BLACK PEPPER

It is rarely that one encounters these days a delicacy that showcases the magic of a single spice — if used imaginatively, it is akin to the keynote in an enticing musical composition. Even black pepper, called the 'king or the queen of spices', constituting the largest volume in international spice trade, has suffered neglect.

Pepper has enjoyed the pride of place for centuries. The quest for a cheap and reliable source of pepper spawning the great exploratory voyages of the 15th and 16th centuries, propelled the spice trade and prepared the way for colonisation of Asia. Different varieties of pepper take their name from the localities they are grown as in — Tellicherry, Alleppey and Malabar. These names come alive in Salman Rushdie's novel *The Moore's Last Sigh* wherein he powerfully evokes the era when pepper trading formed the most important economic activity along the Malabar coast. Chillies, we are told, were brought to India by the Portuguese and it was the good old *marich* (black pepper) or *pipali* (*Piper longum*) that imparted a sharp (*tikshna*) taste to our food so characteristic of the *rajasik* repast, as mentioned in the *Bhagavad Gita.*

According to Ayurveda, *marich* or black pepper provides an effective cure for dyspepsia, tremors, cold and asthma and, believe it or not, the Dutch and the French once used it as a mosquito repellent. Even today it is incorporated in perfumes, lending them an exotic oriental mystique where its presence is almost impossible to discern.

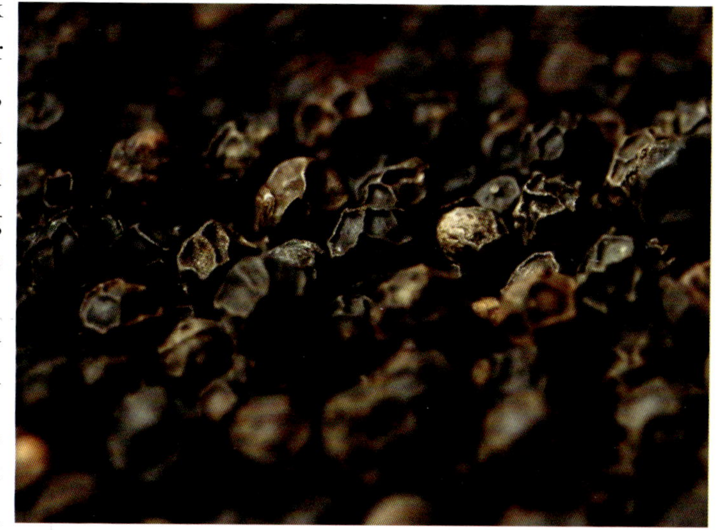

It is perhaps the most common culinary source of seasoning in the West. Pepper, freshly ground, when sprinkled effortlessly and reliably, enlivens a soup, pasta or the fried egg. While it is used quite lavishly in southern culinary styles in

CORIANDER

When the Indian superstar Amitabh Bachchan renders the folk song *'rang barse dhani choonar wali rang barse'* there are not many who are reminded of the poor coriander. The images evoked are of a comely maiden with her clothes drenched with coloured water during the Holi frolic. How easily do we forget that the word *'dhani'* is spawned by the fresh aromatic herb/spice *dhaniya,* aka coriander. *Dhaniya* is called *dhanyak* and the hue *dhani* represents the most refreshing tint of green, symbolising regeneration at the end of a scorching summer in the tropics. Most of us notice it only as an ubiquitous garnishing agent and are reluctant to recognise its culinary significance in Indian cuisine. This seems to be the classic case of intimacy breeding indifference, if not contempt. CTC is indispensable in any *deshi* kitchen and, no, the abbreviation has nothing in common with 'crush tear curl' of the tea-lore; it is shorthand for 'coriander, turmeric and chilli' — the most basic spice combination.

In Chinese or Western cooking, where it is used more sparingly, it is treated with far greater respect. Coriander is one of the oldest spices known to man and archaeological evidence nearly confirmed its use 5,000 years ago. The Hebrews were addicted to cakes flavoured with coriander and the Romans used it to preserve meat. It was Emperor Charlemagne who popularised its cultivation in Europe and by 18th century, coriander seeds coated with sugar were a fashionable sweet and mouth refreshner. In France, it is incorporated in liqueurs like Izarra and Chartereuse and in Mediterranean cooking its contribution is significant, at times crucial, in soups, marinades and pastries. Germans have known it for long and there is a strong tradition of using it liberally in preparing vegetables *a la grecque.* It is also used to season game. Cilantro is a close cousin that is at times confused with coriander. Interestingly, and confusingly, coriander is called Arab or Chinese parsley in France and Greek parsley in Great Britain! The term 'Arab parsley' reminds us of the role played by the Semitic seafarers in the historic spice trade.

Coriander may not be as exotic or expensive as some other spices but its virtues are many. Ayurveda recognises its anti-pyretic, carminative and digestive properties and who can argue about its refreshing flavour? This perhaps is the reason that fresh coriander (paired with mint) is the base of all 'rehydrating', coolant chutneys. The *shuddh shakahari,* who eschew onions, use it with curds to thicken the gravy and in the villages of Uttaranchal, fresh *dhaniya* leaves are ground with chilies and salt to serve to the guest, wishing them an evergreen future. Salt is a prescribed accompaniment with *jaula,* a porridge made with rice and curds, sometimes with black beans. But it is in Kashmir that it is allowed to occupy centre-stage in the delicacy aptly named *dhaniwal qorma.* The dish is aromatic, flavourful and light, without being overpowering. It has a charming personality quite distinct from the more ornate *qormas*, *qaliyas* and *salans* from Awadh, Delhi and Hyderabad. To be honest, we prefer it to the more famous Kashmiri *roghan josh.*

Dhaniwal Korma
(Coriander-flavoured Mutton)

INGREDIENTS

1 kg meat (leg piece)
200 ml of *ghee* or refined oil
200 ml curd
1/4 cup onion paste
2 tsp *sonf* (fennel, powdered)
4 tsp *dhania* (coriander) powder
6 green cardamom
4 cloves
1/4 tsp pepper powder
1/2 turmeric powder
Salt to taste
A bunch of coriander leaves

Method

- Heat the oil in a pan, add the curd and onion paste. Stir well and cook till they blend and the fat separates. Now add the meat, the remaining ingredients and pour three cups of water and boil till the meat becomes tender. Allow it to simmer. Remove from heat.
- Garnish with coriander leaves but resist the temptation to sprinkle the sprigs liberally.
- Remember the spice should sing subtly and the garnishing should not distract the palate.
- One more request before we part — please avoid using pre-powdered and packaged coriander powder for this recipe. Freshly ground coriander seeds release an aroma that nothing else can match.

CARDAMOM

Of all the aromatic spices produced in India, the one most often overlooked is perhaps the cardamom. One associates it more with *paan* (betel leaf) and sweets than with a cooked delicacy. *Launga ilayachi ka beera* is a part of the folklore — now also film songs — and who does not relish it inside the *gulab jamun* or sprinkled on myriad other sweets?

Part of the reason, we feel, is that more often than not, the *panwari*, the *halwai* and the professional cook cut costs by using substandard cardamoms, *kani ilayachi*, with only the shell and no seeds, sans taste and scent and most of us remain unacquainted with the real thing. (Recently, we were pleasantly 'surprised' by a jumbo black cardamom resembling a morel that matched its looks with aroma and flavour.)

How easily do we forget that the cardamom has, in the past, enjoyed unmatched glory? The Chinese mandarins, we are told, chewed the pods when they were granted an audience by the Emperor to ensure that their breath remained fragrant in proximity with the 'Son of Heaven'. In the days gone by, the *nawabs* of Awadh, epitomes of grace and refinement, imbibed green cardamom seeds draped in silver and gold leaves after these were anointed with tobacco-laced rosewater for their 'nicotine fix'. Messers Ittada Khan-Muttada Khan of Lucknow had built an enviable reputation on just one product — their *mushki ilayachidana tambakoo.* The gentry preferred the delicate green cardamom hue for their *sherwani* when regulation black was avoided.

Much before all this had evolved, the etiquette of offering a cardamom to a guest in the court circles of Delhi and Agra existed. The rule was to stretch out one's palm with a few pods on it, never daring to offer a single pod pinched between fingers. The jewellers crafted dainty miniature caskets and barrels in silver and gold to serve as cardamom containers for the nobility.

The connoisseurs of *massala* tea would not exchange cardamom for any other spice — cinnamon or bay leaf — in the brew. Pepper was prescribed as a cure for coughs, not for pleasure.

Though the Europeans are not particularly enamoured by the cardamom and only the Scandinavians use it in some dishes, the Arabs love to marry it with coffee.

A native of Malabar, the *ilayachi-ela* in Sanskrit, has long been famous for its medicinal properties. Ayurvedic texts mention it as a powerful carminative and digestive.

Even in India where it is an indispensable ingredient in the ubiquitous *garam masala,* there are very few recipes in the mainstream that exploit its potential fully. Cardamom is seldom used as a spice on the dominant note or key but it is the 'familiar', hence devalued, aromatic in *pulavs*, *biryani* and *kebab*. (Kerala perhaps is an exception where the traditional stew is redolent with cardamom.) Also, not many seem to appreciate that it is the larger black variety that has a stronger flavour, though the tiny green specimen is valued more!

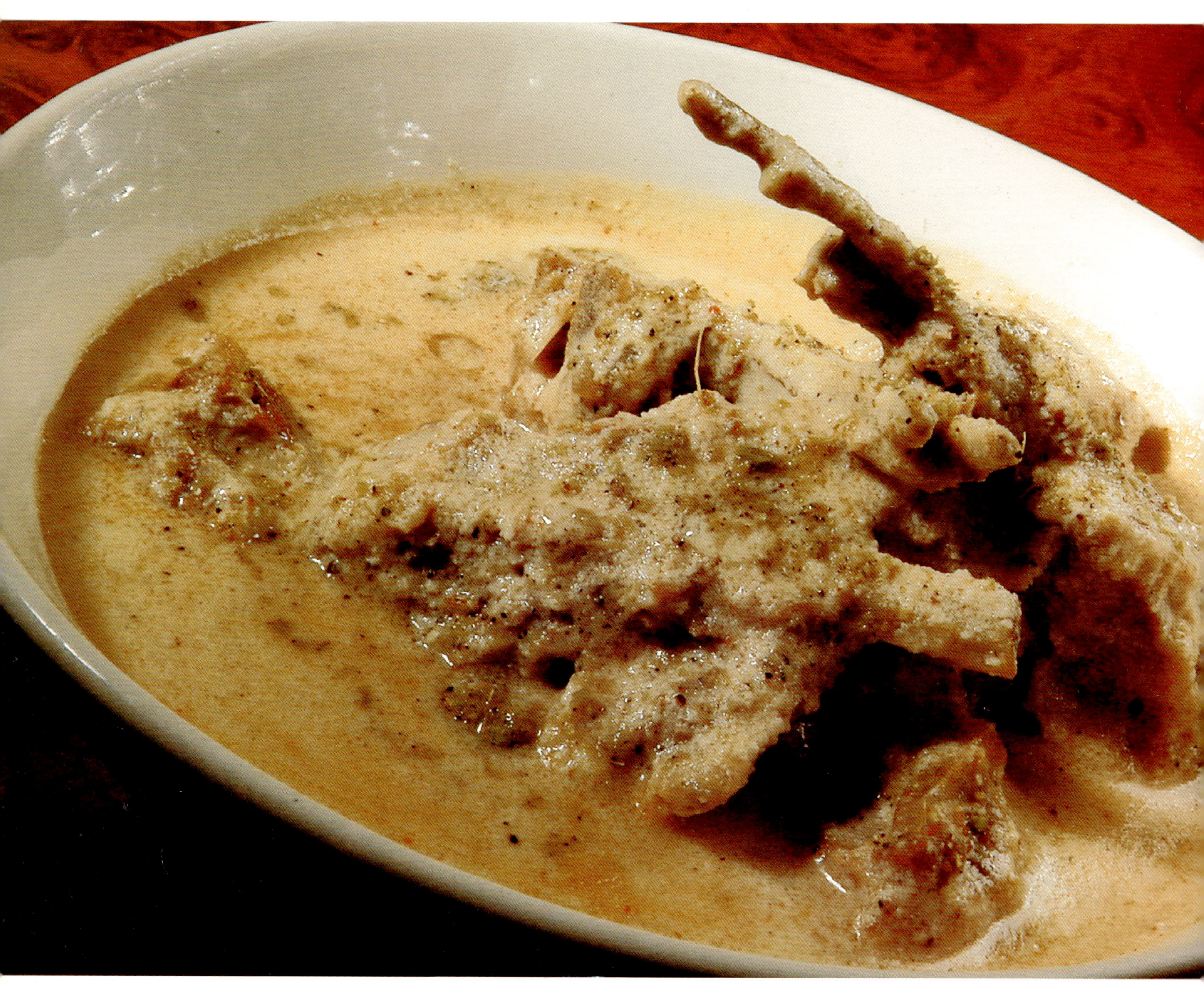

Elayachi Gosht

is a recipe that renders a delightful culinary duet.

Ingredients

1 kg mutton (chops)
125 ml *ghee*
15 green cardamoms
4-6 black cardamoms
50 gm ginger
250 gm onions
6-8 green chillies
500 ml hung yogurt
1 tsp red chilli powder
1 tsp coriander powder
Salt to taste
5 gm cardamom powder
20 gm coriander

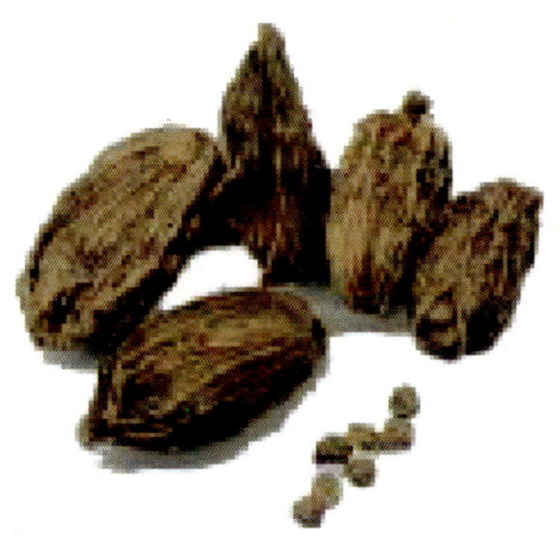

Method

- Wash and trim the meat. Scrape, wash and cut ginger into strips. Clean, wash and chop coriander. Beat the curd with powdered chillies, coriander and salt.
- Heat *ghee* in a pan and put the green and black cardamoms in it. Lightly fry over medium heat until these begin to crackle. Then add the chops, increase to high heat and fry for about five minutes. Lower the flame, add ginger, onions and green chillies and fry for another five minutes (till onions turn lightly brown).
- Then add the curd, stir, bring to a boil, add 4 cups of water and bring to a boil. Cover and reduce the heat to allow it to simmer until the chops are cooked tender.
- Sprinkle cardamom powder. Adjust seasoning.

LEFT
Cardamoms added to mutton-chops enhance the taste of elaychi gosht

KHICHARI

Nowadays when the word '*khichari*' is mentioned, it evokes images of a government formed of ill-matched partners forever restive in an opportunistic alliance. The usage does grave injustice to a historic delicacy. Don't be hasty in raising your eyebrows — today the *khichari* may in popular mind be associated only with convalescence — there was a time when it was the jewel in the Indian culinary crown. Akbar served Salim, his son, the favourite *khichari* to welcome him on his return from a victorious campaign in Deccan. Of course the *shahi khichari* had a regal name to match the recipe — *laziza* (the tasty damsel).

There is an apocryphal story about Birbal, one of the wisest and wittiest courtiers of the Grand Mughal, who took infinitely long to cook the perfect *khichari*. This has become the classic phrase to tease someone about inordinate delay, "*Kya Birbal ki khichari paka rahe ho?*"

Legend has it that during the time of the *nawabs* in Awadh, an exotic *khichari* was prepared by substituting almond slivers for rice and pistachio granules for the green *mung* lentil.

More often than not, a medically prescribed *khichari* combines *mung dal* with ordinary rice and is lightly coloured with turmeric and is supposed to be bland.

To cope with the blandness, *kichari* is usually paired with tangy and piquant partners — *khichari ke char yaar* — *dahi, paapad, ghee, achaar.* Some replace *paapad* with *mooli*. Each to his own.

Khichari also has an important ritual status. When a fast is observed and cereals and grains are taboo, it is better to partake *saboodane ki khichari.* In the month of *Magh,* it is considered obligatory for pious Hindus to eat *mash ki khichari* at least once. The Sahibs during the Raj had *kedgeree* prepared with ingredients like fish, rice and lentils for breakfast. The Hyderabadis love to breakfast with *khichari* and *kheema* and Bengal has its own version of *khichuri* ritually prepared in a celebratory manner, in no way inferior to *pulav* or *biryani.*

The Rajasthanis have an unusual *bajare ki khichari* washed down with large gulps of *lassi*.

Actually *khichari* can be enjoyed at breakfast, lunch and dinner but resist the temptation to cross over into *tahari* or vegetable *pulav* territory. Remember '*pyaar ko pyar hi rahne do, duja naam na do!*' One who has been seduced by *khichari* can look at none else.

A little imagination goes a long way with *khichari*. Substitute yellow *mung* with red or black *masoor* or green *mung* or split *mung* and see how magically it becomes *laziza*. Our own weakness is pronounced for *arhar ki khichari*. Add fresh green chutney and half a spoonful of granular *ghee* — who then will yearn for a loaf of bread, a book of verse, a flask of wine? Omar Khayyam would surely understand, '*khichari*, me and thou, wilderness is paradise now'.

Khichari

Ingredients

Mince (lean meat or boiled yam) 250 gms
Ghee 60 gms
Salt to taste
1 tbs onions ground to paste
1 tsp red chilli powder
½ inch piece ginger grated
1 tsp garlic paste
4 tbsp curd
1 tsp coriander powder, fresh
¼ tsp black cumin seeds
A small pinch each of cinnamon, cardamom and mace powders
100 gms rice
75 gms split green *mung*, husked
½ inch piece ginger, grated
1 tsp garlic paste
30 gms onions very thinly sliced

Method

- Heat *ghee* in a thick-bottomed pan and fry the mince with chillies, garlic, ginger and curds till well browned.
- Add the rest of the *masala* with a little water. Put on *dum* till the mince is tender and dry.

- Heat the *ghee* for the rice in a separate pan. Fry the onions till golden, drain and keep aside. Fry rice and *mung dal* a little with ginger and garlic. Add water and salt and boil till half done. Put on *dum* till cooked three-fourths.
- Spread the rice and lentils over mince meat and put the fired onions on top. Keep on *dum* for another half hour. Sprinkle a little water or milk, if necessary. Blend well before serving hot.

PAAN

No Indian meal is complete without the *paan.* It is considered a digestive agent and leaves a pleasant refreshing after-meal taste. The leaf is believed to be an import from South-east Asia, *circa* 1st century CE. The vine it grows on is called *naagvallari* in Sanskrit literature.

Essentially the *paan* leaf is a 'wrap' which is conical in shape and held secure by a clove, maybe, a convenient receptacle to enclose ingredients for refreshing the breath and titillating the palate. The many varieties of leaf, each commanding a loyal following, are usually identified with reference to a geographical indicator prefixed to their name — *Bangla*, *Mahoba*, *Magahi*, or according to the taste — *meetha*, *saunfiaya*, *gola*, etc. The mini cone is called the *bira* or *veeda* in Sanskrit and *gilouri* in Urdu.

Chuna, lime, and *kattha,* catechu, is a dark hued astringent obtained from the Asian acacia tree. *Chuna,* rich in calcium, is believed to be good for the teeth and *kattha* (*khadir* in Sanskrit) is soothing for sore throat and gum-boils. In the south, *kattha* is mostly dispensed with and *chunam* alone, perhaps aromatised and rose tinted, is enough. In the north-eastern region of India, *chunam* too is not considered an essential and *tambool,* unripened fruit of areca nut provides the heady high and colours the lips with a delightful red.

RIGHT
Paan *eaten after a heavy meal not only helps digestion but also leaves behind a most pleasing and refreshing after-taste on the palate*

Then comes the *supari* or *pugiphal* in Sanskrit. The entire intact nut is considered sacred but edible. It is cut into bite-sized pieces or 'grated' fine

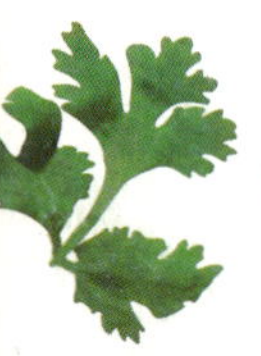

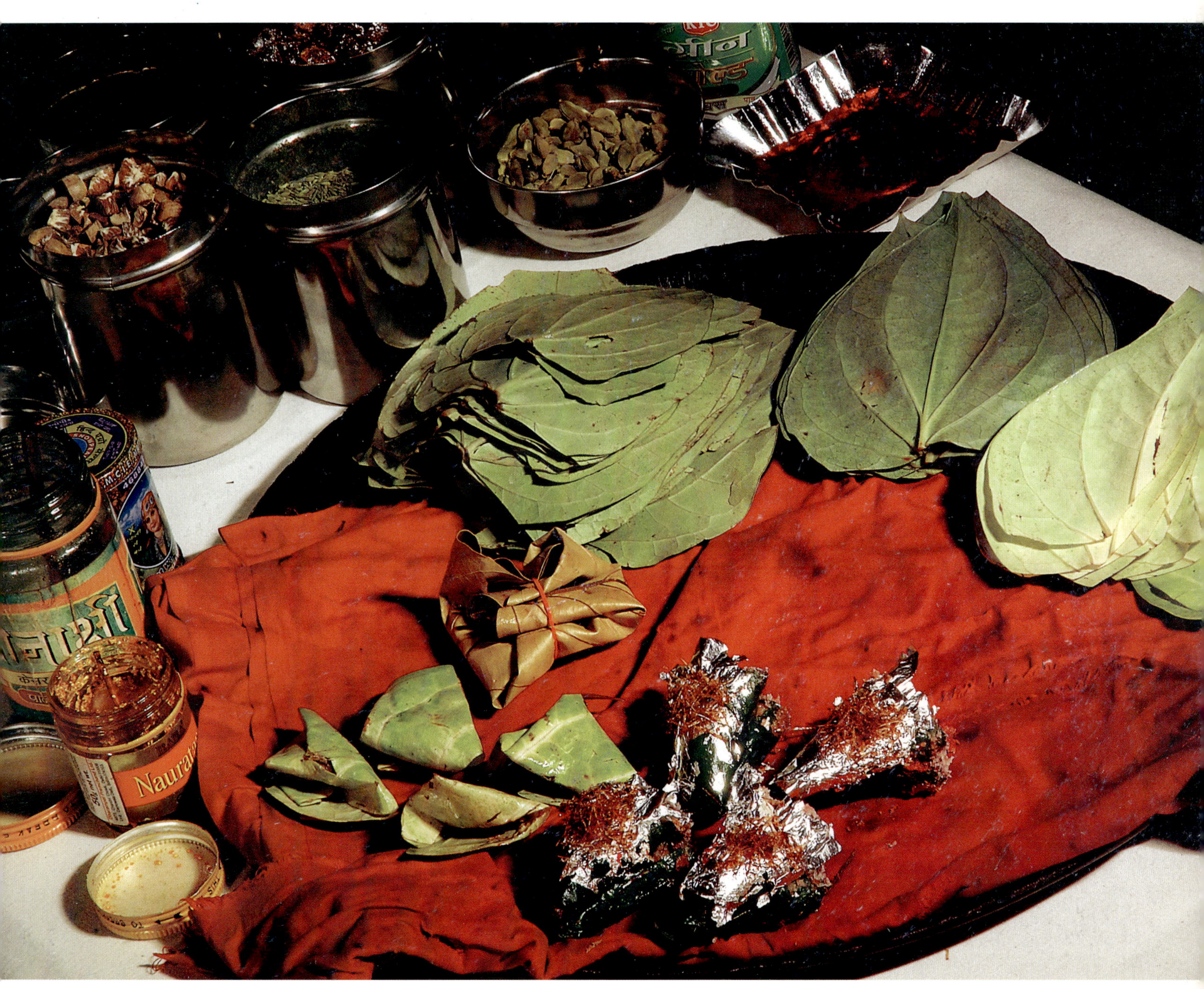

with a *sarauta* to adorn the *paan*. The true *paan* aficionados like their *chhali geeli* softened after soaking in water. In Lucknow, *dakhani supari* is more popular; this is the nut cooked in catechu broth. In Gujarat, it is the *sekeli sopari* (dry and roasted) that reigns supreme.

Many are the aromatic ingredients that enrich the *paan*: cloves, cardamom, fennel, rose petals, *khas*, camphor and saffron. *Saugandhikai* perfumers from Kannauj have traditionally enjoyed a legendary reputation and tobacconists specialising in *paan* have relied upon them.

Meetha paan often replaces the dessert after a heavy meal. It was never a cloyingly sweet confection that is sold at present, overburdened with candied peels and thick syrups of alarming hues. *Misri* or better still, just a touch of cooling *gulqand* or *mulaithi* (liqurice), are what the purists insist upon and should be used to end on a sweet note.